AN UNPRECEDENTED EVIL PERSECUTION

A Genocide Against Goodness in Humankind

Dr. Torsten Trey / Theresa Chu

Clear Insight
Publishing

First Chinese edition (ISBN 978-986-88976-8-7)

Library of Congress Cataloging-in-Publication Data

An Unprecedented Evil Persecution: A Genocide Against Goodness in Humankind / edited by Dr. Torsten Trey and Theresa Chu; translated by the Taiwan International Care Association for Organ Transplants, published by Broad Press Inc. in Taipei in July 2015 pages cm

1. Political persecution 2. Human rights
3. Organ transplant 4. China

First English edition June 2016
ISBN-13: 978-0-9975252-9-8

Library of Congress Control Number: 2016417275

Printed in the United States of America

Published by Clear Insight Publishing, LLC
www.ClearInsightPublishing.com

Cover painting used by special permission of "The Art of Zhen Shan Ren International Exhibition"

Table of Contents

Section III: MEDICINE

Section IV: LAW

Co-Editors' Words

Since publication in 2012, the book State Organs: *Transplant Abuse in China*, has been translated and published internationally, receiving positive feedback from medical and legal professionals, experts in various fields of business, and politicians. The book was co-edited by David Matas, Nobel Peace Prize Nominee and Canadian human rights lawyer, and Dr. Trey, Executive Director of Doctors Against Forced Organ Harvesting (DAFOH). Many people, while initially incredulous over these startling reports, are now facing the reality of China's state-sanctioned organ harvesting of living prisoners of conscience. Forums and hearings intended to expose and end the government's crimes have been held in many places, including the U.S. Congress and the European Parliament. Chinese citizens behind the iron curtain have risked their lives to sign a petition calling for action to stop these crimes. However, the Chinese Communist Party (CCP) continues to practice live organ harvesting.

An echo after the publication of State Organs revealed another aspect. It became obvious that the root beneath the forced organ harvesting as a profitable transplant market was a genocide the Chinese government committed against its own citizens—Falun Gong practitioners. In China they are reported to be the largest victim group used for sourcing of organs and to be the primary target of illegal forced organ harvesting precisely for the reason that they are highly vulnerable, persecuted, marginalized and ostracized. Discussions on an international level have made it clear: as long as the Falun Gong are the target of widespread persecution they will remain the primary source, and the crimes of live organ harvesting will continue.

Seeing a need to look into the root cause in order to stop the forced organ harvesting, Dr. Trey invited human rights activist and attorney, Ms. Chu, Esq., to join him in co-editing a new book that exposes and discusses the persecution of the Falun Gong in China and how it has played a vital role in the CCP's organ harvesting crimes. Together they solicited analysis from renowned scholars, politicians, lawyers, physicians, artists and human rights activists who are long-time observers of China and the CCP's crimes against humanity. The massive campaign to vilify and annihilate the peaceful, popular Falun Gong and the coinciding skyrocketing success of China's transplant business was initiated under former Chinese Party Chief Jiang Zemin in July 1999. The book describes the global scope and impact from political, sociological, economical, medical, legal, journalistic, and cultural perspectives.

The objective analysis by 19 co-authors from Europe, North America, Australia and Asia offers the reader an opportunity to learn that the genocide of Falun Gong is not merely a campaign against 100 million practitioners who seek to cultivate themselves. This persecution has severely damaged the conscience and goodwill of human beings all over the world, and by trying to implicate every one of us in this unprecedented evil, has expanded into a threat against the very goodness inherent in humankind. If left unchecked, the extent of its impact is beyond our imagination.

The title, *An Unprecedented Evil Persecution*, is an apt description of these atrocious crimes against humanity. The book is a solemn call to awaken our conscience. We must all do what we can to preserve the best of our humanity and end this human rights catastrophe that is unprecedented in its scale.

Section I

MEDIA

A Dictator's Logic

By Michel Wu

In October 1999, Alain Peyrefitte, Editorial Director of *Le Figaro*, one of the largest newspapers in France, conducted a written interview with then head of the Chinese Communist Party (CCP), Jiang Zemin, prior to his visit to France. The written interview asked for Jiang's comments on issues in China, France and other parts of the world.

Jiang, in an attempt to justify his launch of the violent persecution against Falun Gong half a year before, seized this opportunity to proactively control the international media by naming Falun Gong an "evil cult."

The CCP picked France for two reasons. First, after the *Order of the Solar Temple* incident that shocked the world, France had been adopting a series of administrative and judicial measures for many years to prevent cults from proliferating within the country. Therefore, the CCP saw this unique historical period as a good opportunity to instigate confusion between good and bad.

The second reason is that interviews with visiting foreign dignitaries are intensely sought after by the French media in the fierce competition for the consumer market. The CCP played the game by giving *Le Figaro* the privilege to interview Jiang on the condition that the interview text must be published in full. Peyrefitte, who loved the political and media spotlight, was obedient to the CCP's demands.

On the day of Jiang's arrival in France, *Le Figaro* published the entire content of his interview as previously agreed. The interview severely impacted local public opinion: Some journalists mindlessly parroted Jiang's words while others remained silent, afraid to make the slightest noise about the ongoing arrest, detention, torture, and brainwashing against Falun Gong in mainland China.

By the early 90's, the CCP had already ruled China for over 40 years, resulting in immense suffering for hundreds of millions of innocent people. Chinese citizens in general began to cast doubt on the Communist ideology and many were looking for a renewed connection to their traditional, spiritual roots. Falun Gong, a self-improvement practice of the Buddhist School, based on truthfulness, compassion and forbearance, received widespread recognition throughout all levels of Chinese society in a surprisingly short period of time. The CCP's official media promoted Falun Gong as "100 percent beneficial and not a bit harmful." By 1998, six years after its introduction to the public, up to 100 million people—by the government's own estimates—have practiced Falun Gong. As the practice grew in popularity, however, the CCP started to change its view of Falun Gong.

Ever since the CCP came into power, it has strictly maintained an essential principle: it must never allow the parallel existence of other organizations. The CCP considers the top-down vertical rule as the fundamental necessity for its survival. The so-called "People's Political Consultative Conference" is merely window-dressing. Members must declare their loyalty to the CCP in their Party Constitutions. From the "People's Representative Conference" to community organizations such as the Labor Union, Communist Youth League, Women's Federation, and other organizations in factories, schools, shops, neighborhoods and villages, all have to establish CCP committees or sub-committees. This is the characteristic of China's political reality. With Falun Gong now prominently positioned on the national stage, with more adherents than there were in the CCP itself, the practice unintentionally served to threaten the government's survival. The principles that the practice promotes are diametrically opposite to the Party principles, yet, before the crackdown, it was received with adoration and esteem by hundreds of millions of people including CCP members. In light of the upheaval in the Soviet Union and other Eastern European regions just a few years prior, the CCP became overly fearful and regarded the apolitical Falun Gong like Poland's Solidarnos Union.

When the CCP concluded that Falun Gong posed a significant threat to its power, frenzied and barbaric oppression ensued. After the 1989 Tiananmen Square massacre, a new large group of innocent people had become the CCP's primary target of persecution. Similar to past political movements, there were mass arrests all across the nation. Detention, imprisonment, and brainwashing were preceded by defamation filled with lies. The goal was to use false accusation to coerce the people, who were ignorant of the facts, to join in with the CCP and "destroy" Falun Gong from all fronts and within all strata.

I started my university studies in 1956. Like many of my young friends, I enjoyed playing basketball. We decided to organize a basketball match among the classes. Before the start of the first game, an older student appeared on the basketball court. He sternly questioned us, "What are you all doing?" I politely answered that we were having a basketball match. "Basketball match? Did you get approval from the Party sub-committee?" I told him that we did not. He immediately reprimanded us, "The Party sub-committee does not know? Dismiss!" That was when we found out that this student was a Party official before he entered the university and that he was also the freshman secretary of the Party sub-committee. It was my introduction to the organizational rule of the Party.

A year later, an editorial titled *"Why is this?"* published by the CCP's official newspaper People's Daily, was the trigger of the "anti-rightist" campaign. Stories about those "anti-Party, anti-socialism rightists" were published continuously. Twenty years later, I met up with a "rightist" classmate. After a bit of chitchat, I found out that he was a "rightist" no more. He gave me a wry smile and said, "Yeah, they have removed my dunce cap once again."

The start of the Cultural Revolution in 1966 was triggered by a critique on a historical play. One day, after Mao's Red Guards took over the Xinhua News Agency's editorial department, I inadvertently met up with Mu Qing, Xinhua's editorial chief who had been physically attacked as a "demonic animal" and sentenced to "reeducation through labor" for his subversive politics. Curious for more information about this, I asked him, "How did you get on the Capitalism path?" He answered with a bit of confusion, "Me? Thirty years as a Communist revolutionist and I didn't understand Marx and Lenin…"

On the evening of June 3, 1989, the first day of the student protests, I called Beijing from Paris to inquire: "What is actually happening? Who are the Tiananmen Square hoodlums?" The crisp response before the call terminated was: "Don't ask. The military is already in control of the headquarters!" Every time before an important political movement, the first thing that happens is absolute media control. This is the general modus operandi of a totalitarian regime.

The anti-Falun Gong media campaign started on June 17, 1996 by China's *Guangming Daily*. Over a dozen newspapers and magazines followed suit. On July 23, 1999, *People's Daily*, issued an editorial that read: "Raise your awareness. See clearly the danger. Hold firm to the policy. Safeguard stability." Using stern language, the editorial alleged that Falun Gong was an "illegal organization." From there, the bugle sounded to suppress and eradicate Falun Gong. At the same time, the CCP mobilized religious, civic and academic organizations already under its control, to give anti-Falun Gong speeches and hold anti-Falun Gong conferences. And so, a nameless crime was created under organized and orchestrated verbal and written attacks, leading to an unprecedented tragic political movement.

The names used by the CCP against Falun Gong changed constantly, from "illegal organization" to "cult group" to "reactionary hostile organization" to "Western anti-China political instrument" to "anti-government organization" to "reactionary political group and political force" to "terrorist organization." All the irresponsible propaganda caused my French colleagues quite a bit of confusion.

I bid farewell to Xinhua Agency after the June 4, 1989 Beijing tragedy and accepted an invitation from the Board of Directors of the Radio France Internationale (RFI) to start up a Chinese branch in France, with the purpose of targeting a mainland Chinese audience. Shortly after Jiang's visit to France, the Chinese Embassy sent someone to talk to the Chairman of RFI, Jean Paul Cluzel, about the Chinese broadcasting branch. Cluzel requested that the manager of the Chinese branch should also join the meeting. The Beijing diplomat adamantly rejected the proposal. After the meeting, Cluzel said with a smile, "I have just met a Red Guard."

Shortly thereafter, another Beijing diplomat invited me for coffee. He did not beat around the bush: "What I want to talk to you about is the Falun Gong issue. Do not report Falun Gong in the Chinese program you are in charge of." I asked him why. Without hesitation, he said, "Falun Gong is a cult, I brought you a lot of materials." From underneath the table, he pulled out a large bag filled with anti-Falun Gong materials, brochures, posters, videos and CDs.

I told him clearly: "Cult is the name you use. RFI is an independent media. Without any independent investigation, we cannot write reports on Falun Gong, nor can we make reports based on what you say."

I suggested that, "Since the Falun Gong issue has been politicized and internationalized, the mainland Chinese authorities should open the door and let the international media conduct independent investigations on the Falun Gong issue."

Shortly after Jiang's visit to France, my colleagues and I found a special column that targeted the Falun Gong issue on the Embassy's website. This spare-no-effort fervor, which continues to include diplomacy outlets to negatively target Falun Gong, may deceive people for a time, but most certainly would raise a red flag, keep people on alert, and in doubt.

Jiang used *Le Figaro* to influence public opinion and deceive the people of France, yet he could not stop the French authorities and the intellectually-curious from exploring the facts about Falun Gong. The French government issued a decree in November, 2002 and established the *Mission Interministerielle de Vigilance et de Lutte contre les Derives Sectaires* panel directly under the Prime Minister's Office. Its mission is to "be vigilant and fight against the proliferation of cults" and to "observe and analyze the cult phenomenon through their actions against human rights and fundamental freedoms." The task force is also responsible for "coordinating public empowerment to prevent and repress various cult actions."

The French government has not listed Falun Gong as a cult to be watched and suppressed. To this day, every weekend without exception, Falun Gong practitioners gather in front of the Eiffel

Tower and two other parks to do group exercises. Their Tian Guo Marching Band continues to participate in large cultural activities organized by the government. Moreover, Falun Gong practitioners have held several informational conferences and forums in the French People's Parliament Building to help people understand the true side of Falun Gong and the persecution.

Falun Gong's applications to hold silent protests in front of the Chinese Embassy, however, have consistently been denied by the French police department with one excuse after another. In July 2009, Falun Gong practitioners sued the French police authority. In the end, the Paris Administrative Court, le tribunal administratif de Paris, ruled in favor of Falun Gong and ordered the French police to pay 1,000 euros as compensation to the French Falun Dafa Association.

Indeed, without sufficient knowledge of the Chinese traditional culture and having no insight of the modern Communist state, it is difficult for foreigners to immediately understand the truth about Falun Gong. Among the many victimized groups during different periods of the CCP's history, Falun Gong is unusual, neither being crushed nor dispersed under the weight of such heavy propaganda and brutal persecution. In the resistance against tyranny, Falun Gong was the first to reveal the true history and nature of the CCP through the publication, *Nine Commentaries on the Communist Party*. While under severe persecution, Falun Gong blazed a refreshingly new path in Chinese journalism by establishing, outside of China, the Epoch Times newspaper, *Sound of Hope* radio station, *New Tang Dynasty Television* (NTDTV), and a large number of other independent media.

I am convinced that Falun Gong, as an atypical group against tyranny, will be able to fulfill its dreams of "bringing kindness back to the human world and returning the mountains and rivers to clarity" as long as these practitioners, who have been thrown onto the main stage of history, maintain a pure heart, and stay away from the secular dust.

Moreover, with unprecedented courage and firm moral conviction, Falun Gong practitioners have exposed the CCP's unconscionable actions to international organizations and brought lawsuits against many CCP leaders in foreign courts. Recently, Falun Gong practitioners founded the Shen Yun Performing Arts Company with the mission to promote traditional Chinese culture, and have also organized multiple international arts and cultural competitions. Falun Gong practitioners are joining ranks with all victims of communism, with a commitment to combat this repressive system of control until all people, particularly the people in China, are liberated and able to enjoy the freedoms of a democratic society.

Soon after the persecution of Falun Gong began, a group of common people that has come to be known as "petitioners" became a unique focal point in Beijing. Under the cover of China's economic successes under the one-party monopoly, these people have been oppressed by corrupt officials, their families have been broken up and there is nowhere for them to redress their grievances. Year after year, taking great risks, they continue to flock to Beijing, hoping to petition and plead for a bit of justice. The result is, these petitioners are often shut out, and even thrown into black jails. Many worry that these petitioners are the last batch of Chinese victims under communism. The political label that the CCP put on this group still has not been removed.

These so-called gentlemen of the society choose to ignore the evil of communism, refuse to help those in danger, and yet, they speak up to justify totalitarianism, and are even eager to share a piece of the communist action. I wonder if they have ever thought that this momentary glory will bring them and their future generations eternal disgrace?!

Alain Peyrefitte is believed to be a person who had been "charmed by Zhou Enlai— former head of state under communist rule— and unable to extricate himself. " After his death, the CCP erected a statue of him on the Wuhan University campus for students to pay their respects. But, what do China's young people remember about him? In addition to acting as an accomplice of Jiang— contributing to the suffering of millions—he published a book of Chinese propaganda in 1973, *When China Awakes, the World Will Tremble*. The book attempts to sensationalize China during the epileptic time of the Cultural Revolution. Those close to Peyrefitte commented that the China he depicted was the China described by Enlai. The author argued that with an enormous population and considerable economic and technological strength, China would gain a foothold in the world. In response to Peyrefitte's premise, a reader wrote the following: "If democracy is not embraced, if communist dictatorship is not abandoned, China's emergence as a superpower is merely a fool's errand."

Total Media Monopoly:
The Effective and Successful Manipulation of Even the Most Critical and Skeptical Opponents of the Chinese Party/State

By Clive Ansley, BA, MA, LL.B, and LL.M

I lived and worked in China for fourteen years and from 1999 to 2003 I observed firsthand the vicious campaign of vilification and demonization unleashed by the Chinese Communist Party ("CCP") and its then General Secretary, Jiang Zemin. In those early days, no one could possibly have contemplated or foreseen the nightmarish and diabolical designs that Jiang and a small fiendish cabal surrounding him were fashioning as a "final solution" to the threat they attributed to the peaceful practitioners of Falun Gong.

Today, the reality of the mass murder and organ pillaging from the practitioners of Falun Gong by the CCP cannot be questioned. The massive evidence from unimpeachable sources compels us to take the *Slaughter* as a given. But looking back, what is there about the Chinese political system, which might possibly account for the fact that since 1999 an atrocity, which in some ways dwarfs the atrocities committed by the Third Reich, has continued unabated in China?

How did this come about? What made it possible? With the benefit of hindsight, it seems clear that the astonishing and hysterical campaign of hatred and vitriol released against Falun Gong by Jiang Zemin was intended to numb the sensibilities of those who would be called upon to commit the cruelest atrocities and tortures against their fellow man in the name of heroic struggle against an "evil cult" (Not the Chinese Communist Party, but *another* alleged "evil cult"!).

Juxtaposing a distinguishing feature of both Nazi Germany and today's China—a once civil and rational society becoming overrun by "a ruthless political party … careful to hide its criminal activities from [the] public eye"—the Judgment of an Israeli Ecclesiastical Court noted the eerily similar way both persecutions have been received by the world community. [1]

The Goebbels theory of the "Big Lie" is too well known to warrant elaboration. Tell it often enough and make it big enough and people will believe it. The Third Reich made full use of this principle in its demonization of the Jews. They succeeded in portraying the Jews as a kind of sub-species, not quite human, and a dangerous threat to German society.

This is what I witnessed the CCP do to the Falun Gong. It should surprise no one that the models for many CCP policies and campaigns are to be found in Nazi Germany. The so-called "Communist" Party of China is communist in name only. In reality, it perfectly conforms to the classical definition of fascism.

The campaign I witnessed unfolding against the Falun Gong in those early years of the persecution even then reminded me daily of the Nazi demonization of the Jews. But I could never have foreseen the horrific revelations to come.

Ironically, the massive media vilification of Falun Gong in those days regularly falsely accused Falun Gong practitioners of the very kinds of inhuman and obscene crimes we now know the CCP continues to perpetrate against Falun Gong practitioners, human rights lawyers, dissidents, Christians, Uighurs, and Tibetans.

It was Jiang Zemin who at the very beginning of the persecution coined the characterization of Falun Gong as an "evil cult". In order to fan the flames of hatred against this latest group in a long line of victims targeted by the CCP over the course of its history, the CCP published stories of Falun Gong practitioners killing their children, even going so far as to claim that the practitioners actually ate their children!

The inflammatory horror stories and fairy tales carried daily in the print and television media in those early years gave visceral shape and content to the growing personification of the "evil cult" whose image the CCP was manufacturing and disseminating.

A story widely covered in the Chinese media involved an individual who had put rat poison in the noodles at a popular restaurant in Nanjing. Forty-two people had died. These murders were attributed to the teachings of Falun Gong. Though I knew nothing about Falun Gong at that time, I did not believe this story for an instant. For one thing, I got the very strong impression that saddling Falun Gong with responsibility for this mass murder had been essentially an afterthought on the part of the Chinese authorities. The "trial" of the alleged murderer had been well publicized and there had been no mention of Falun Gong in the coverage of that event. But as he was being taken away for execution, the media seemed to be adding the message that "By the way, he was a Falun Gong practitioner." I remember clearly that most of the story had already unfolded before any allegation of a Falun Gong link had been crafted.

In these early days, it seems I never saw any media report not filled with savage hatred directed against Falun Gong, usually accompanied by tales of diabolical and inhuman practices allegedly resulting from the study of Falun Gong.

Again, though I had no knowledge of Falun Gong during the early years of the persecution, I was highly skeptical of the CCP's accusations. The Falun Gong victims of the CCP defamation were of course denied any forum through which to answer the accusations against them. But I know from long personal experience that China under the CCP is based on institutional lying. This is true to the point that lying by CCP leaders, party and government organs, and spokespersons is virtually pathological. They are incapable of speaking the truth, even when the truth is not harmful to them. The CCP lies on general principles, even when there is no reason to hide the truth. A joke so widespread in China that it has become a cliché holds that "The only true statement in the *People's Daily* is the date." So I was a skeptic.

Why was it possible for the CCP to sell the "Big Lie" to so many of the Chinese citizenry?

This is not a simple question. It is a puzzling one, precisely because of the seemingly overwhelming lack of credibility from which the CCP suffers in the eyes of most Chinese. The CCP is widely hated in China for many reasons. And quite aside from hatred, it is widely understood to lack any semblance of credibility. So how does it happen that the CCP can continually launch persecutions against supposed pariahs and cause much of the Chinese population to fall into line?

The observation that China is a complex and multi-faceted society is a hackneyed one. But it is fundamental to understanding the seemingly inexplicable contradiction between the widespread disrespect for and fear of the CCP on the one hand, and the repeated successes the CCP enjoys on the other hand with so many of its propaganda campaigns.

I believe we can identify at least some of the factors giving rise to these puzzling contradictions. First, like all fascist states, China profits hugely by skillfully catering to jingoism and nationalism. Creating imaginary threats to the nation, both external and internal, is a tried and tested method. The history of imperialist aggression and predation in China by western powers has produced a rather schizoid attitude toward those western powers. The CCP has been remarkably successful in harnessing China's wounded pride, which persists as a corrosive legacy of her victimization by the imperialist invaders during the nineteenth and twentieth centuries.

Chinese who detest the CCP regularly rally behind its leaders to support anti-American demonstrations or territorial claims against Tibet, Taiwan, and virtually any island in the East or South China Seas.

Similarly, with respect to domestic issues I knew many individuals who regularly ridiculed the CCP for habitual lying, yet swallowed the party line on particular issues, without blinking.

Close to 100% of Chinese citizens, for example, appear to support capital punishment. When I argued against it on the basis that execution of the innocent is inevitable, I was almost always greeted with incredulity. Typically, I was told that no one on trial for a capital crime in China was innocent, because the Chinese police would never charge anyone who was not guilty. But the very people making this argument were often the most strident critics of the CCP and the entire Chinese system! They were the very people who most often attacked the credibility of the CCP, yet the fact that the CCP exercises micro-management over both the police and the courts apparently never occurred to them.

Almost all lawyers with whom I worked in China regularly invoked the joke about the date being the only truth in the *People's Daily*. But I vividly remember discussing with one such lawyer the story of an alleged Falun Gong follower killing her two children. At that time, knowing nothing of Falun Gong, I did not argue that the story was necessarily false. I simply questioned why we should believe it, given the source.

The discussion had been sparked by a comment from this lawyer that Falun Gong practitioners were "terrible people". I asked him why he was so sure of this. He responded with the example of a double infanticide by a Falun Gong mother. "But", I asked him, "How do you know that that is true, that it really happened?" He responded that he had just watched a full television newscast about the killing the previous evening (as had I!). I then reminded him of who controls China Central Television ("CCTV"). He is a person who had regularly argued that no one should believe anything they see in the CCP media; yet now he was insisting to me that Falun Gong is clearly evil and basing his argument on a television program passed by the censors of the CCP's Central Propaganda Unit, at a time when the CCP was mounting another massive campaign against yet another alleged "enemy of the people".

I had a similar discussion with another CCP critic and skeptic over the alleged restaurant poisoner in Nanjing. Again, this lady was angrily denouncing the Falun Gong after having read in the newspapers and seen on television the claims that the person to be executed had been a Falun Gong practitioner and had committed his crimes as a result of the practice.

When five alleged Falun Gong practitioners apparently attempted a group suicide by self-immolation in Tiananmen Square, the event received saturation coverage in both the print and TV media. It was very effective. My observation at the time was that most Chinese who saw the stories were disgusted with Falun Gong as a result.

Even I accepted the "fact" that these self-immolations had occurred and that the news coverage was legitimate. Unlike almost all other anti-Falun Gong stories I had seen, this one carried live footage and I witnessed the horrifying event "with my own eyes". It did not turn me against Falun Gong, for several reasons, but I never at the time entertained any doubt that the event was real and the media coverage genuine. Only several years later did I have the opportunity to view compelling evidence that the entire event had been a hoax staged by the Beijing police.

Everyone familiar with the persecution of Falun Gong now knows what really happened. The film footage was genuine, but what it covered was not. The five who doused themselves with gasoline and set themselves on fire were clearly shown not to be Falun Gong practitioners; every one of the five "protesters" had police standing behind them with fire extinguishers ready to use within seconds; and the clothing of all five was visibly bulked up with what now appear to have been fire retardant materials. Also later came the realization that the nearest fire extinguishers would ordinarily be far removed from the center of Tiananmen Square. There is no way that ten police officers could have reached the demonstration with fire extinguishers in time to douse the flames, unless the whole exercise had been staged and pre-planned.

But we did not think of those things at the time. I did not argue back then that the event had been staged. My arguments with Chinese lawyers and others were limited to the observation first, that every organization and movement attracts some extremists and we do not condemn Christianity when some unbalanced mother in the U.S. drowns her five children in the bathtub because "Jesus told me to do it"; second, this act could have been a reflection of the utter desperation felt by people driven over the edge by the persecution; third, similar self-immolations by Buddhist monks in Vietnam in the early 1960's and more recently in Tibet have been hailed as acts of incredible heroism and self-sacrifice.

One lesson we have learned from the persecution in China, and from the media campaigns which have facilitated that persecution is this: Even a people who have purportedly learned to place no credibility on anything carried by their state monopolized media can still be repeatedly duped and manipulated by that same media in certain instances. If the "Big Lie" is repeated without respite; if the monopoly of the media is absolute so that no response by the accused is possible; if a jingoistic appeal to national pride is carried incessantly or fears of either external or internal enemies are exploited; then even a populace which considers itself too sophisticated to be taken in by the state propaganda organs will in fact be so taken in, time and time again.

Westerners must try to imagine the effects on a population when 100% of their print and broadcast media are subject to a total monopoly of all information. Citizens develop an overall and general cynicism, but are prone to being repeatedly deceived about specific issues or events which are presented to them from only one monotone viewpoint. The persecution of Falun Gong over the past fifteen years is an excellent case in point.

Our Western media is also very venal in many ways. Certainly individual media organs in Canada and the U.S. represent special vested interests and weight their news coverage to benefit those special vested interests. But the absence of an absolute monopoly over the media, and especially the absence of a state monopoly, means the object of any character assassination normally can find a way to reply and get an opposing view into the public eye.

We must never underestimate the power of even a widely disrespected propaganda machine, when it is the only available source of information or opinion. There were undoubtedly neighbors who knew that the accused mother was not a Falun Gong practitioner or even that she did not kill her children. Any Falun Gong practitioners could have told any media interviewer that nothing in the teachings of Falun Gong sanctions any kind of killing. Undoubtedly there were people in Nanjing who could have provided evidence that the mass poisoner there had never been a Falun Gong practitioner. Falun Gong practitioners could easily have pointed out that no practitioner ever adopts the sitting position of the alleged self-immolators in Tiananmen Square.

But how would anyone have pointed out any of these things? How would anyone have placed an alternate theory before the public? There was no possible avenue open to them. They could not have letters to the editor published; they could not write opinion pieces for the op-ed page; they could not give interviews on television news programs. They could not even rally in public with placards. Only one voice was ever heard. When this one singular view on any issue is repeated *ad nauseam*, day in and day out, and no dissenting voice is ever heard, no reply is ever forthcoming, then the very people who have counseled us never to believe anything from the CCP media begin to believe the message in spite of themselves.

When Falun Gong practitioners were accused, they had no forum in which to respond. Whether guilty as charged or victims of vicious defamation, the response of the Falun Gong practitioners never reached the Chinese public.

Moreover, in the early years of the persecution, citizens were not left to passively imbibe and ingest the CCP hate campaign against Falun Gong. The many media accounts at the time of mass rallies to denounce the practice and make public criticisms of practitioners was hauntingly reminiscent of earlier historical precedents such as the anti-landlord campaigns, the anti-Rightist campaigns, the Cultural Revolution, the anti-Confucius and Anti-Lin Biao campaigns. Such campaigns have always been designed to help the CCP transform passive readers or listeners into active participants in the hate campaign of the day.

Actual physical participation in persecution seems to be very effective psychologically. The participant is taken to a higher stage

of commitment because of his or her own complicity. During
the Cultural Revolution it was not uncommon for wives to take
part in the public condemnation and severe beating of their own
husbands, in order to demonstrate their own political purity and
loyalty to the movement. Both in that period and in the course of
the persecution against the Falun Gong, actual participation has
served to some extent as a protection against becoming a target
of the campaign.

Public denunciations and arbitrary beatings by police, forfeitures
of property and bank accounts, employers being forced to
fire anyone identified as a practitioner of Falun Gong, routine
and arbitrary "administrative" detentions and imprisonment
of practitioners, all these things served to reinforce the tacit
acceptance that practitioners of Falun Gong were somehow
"not quite human" and need not be accorded the basic respect to
which human beings are normally entitled. All these things have
played a role in rendering Chinese police, paramilitary, medical
personnel, and prison guards amenable to committing murder,
diabolical torture, and the most gruesome crimes against
humanity the world has seen since the Holocaust. I refer of
course to the mass murder of healthy human beings, kept alive
in donor herds, to be slaughtered on demand so their organs can
be sold by the state at huge profits.

We must remember that the Chinese population as a whole has
never been told about the atrocious and inhuman crimes the CCP
has perpetrated against the practitioners of Falun Gong, just as
the Nazis never publicly acknowledged the Death Camps. The
function of the dehumanization and demonization campaigns
against both the Jews and the Falun Gong practitioners did not
in either case involve the public as a whole; it rather served to
anesthetize the agents of the state who would be enlisted to
actually commit the atrocities. The screams of the victims tend
to fall on deaf ears when the perpetrators of the atrocities can

rationalize that the dying victims are, after all, "only Jews", or only "members of an evil cult".

The success of this campaign to dehumanize Falun Gong practitioners is perhaps nowhere better exemplified than in the co-opting of the country's medical profession. Outside of contemporary China and Nazi Germany, who could ever conceive of a medical profession whose members actually willingly take part in the routine murder of healthy human beings who have never been condemned even by a Chinese "court", let alone a real court? Outside of Germany in the 1930's and contemporary China, who could conceive of "murder committees" comprised jointly of doctors in transplant hospitals and "judges" in Chinese criminal "courts" who cooperate in arranging for the killing of compatible "donors" in order to supply fresh organs to waiting wealthy customers? But that is the reality of the medical profession in China today. Would this be possible in the absence of the concerted campaign by the CCP to de-humanize the adherents of Falun Gong? It is doubtful.

China, as anyone who is familiar with the country can attest, is not a state subject to "rule of law". The law is whatever the tyrant of the day says it is. Falun Gong was declared an "evil cult" and made eligible for "prosecution" through the vehicle of a simple edict from Jiang Zemin. Yet, there was and is no section of the Chinese Criminal Code which could be stretched under any legitimate legal regime so as to apply to Falun Gong. Even if there were, the "courts" were never asked to interpret the law and hear evidence. The oligarch of the hour simply declared all practitioners guilty and proceeded with the persecution.

Surely the very existence of mass murder for organ pillage, as an ongoing atrocity, renders ludicrous any pretensions that China is a country ruled by law. Yet, the CCP since 1979 has made every effort to promote the appearance of a *bona fide* legal system, just as did the Nazis during the era of the Third Reich. It is crucially important to oppressors in totalitarian states that they are able to point to the apparent form of a legal system and claim that all their actions are rooted in law.

The most telling facts exposing the truly fraudulent nature of the Chinese "legal system" are that the Chinese "courts" are forbidden by the CCP from accepting any lawsuits from Falun Gong practitioners contesting their loss of constitutional rights, and all Chinese lawyers are forbidden to undertake legal representation of any Falun Gong practitioners.

The patently false representation that China is a state governed by the "rule of law" and that Chinese "courts" are independent has served as an essential tool in the cultivation of respect for China abroad. This tool has been employed widely both by the CCP itself and by its handmaidens in those Western governments heavily tilted toward the CCP.

Two previous Canadian Prime Ministers, both close friends of the CCP leaders responsible for the worst of China's human rights abuses, routinely trumpeted the alleged "legal reforms" which they falsely claimed, to Canadian citizens, were unfolding in China. In the third year of the persecution, Jean Chretien stood shoulder to shoulder with Jiang Zemin and extolled the "...tremendous advances in human rights which have taken place over the last ten years under the leadership of President Jiang. "His successor, Paul Martin, did not go to quite such ridiculous lengths, but continued to praise China's alleged progress in human rights and its commitment to implementing the "rule of law". Neither has ever addressed the fundamental truth that both in theory and in practice, the CCP ranks above the law and exercises total control over all organs of the legal system, including police, prosecutors, "courts", and interpretation of statutes.

China can have a "legal" system controlled by the CCP or it can have the "rule of law"; it is conceptually impossible to have both.

So long as the CCP maintains the external form and structure of a genuine legal system, it enables the Chretiens and Martins of the West to ignore the substance of the system and continue their misrepresentations to their citizens about the alleged steady progress in advancing the "rule of law" in China.

So long as the CCP remains in power, it is difficult to imagine the persecution and the forced organ harvesting coming to an end any time soon. But for this to happen, it is necessary to make the existence of these crimes fully known to the Chinese people and to the people of the world.

---

[1] Judgment of the Ecclesiastical Sanhedrin Court in Jerusalem, July 15, 2008

Suppressing the Truth is the Root of all Evil

By Chang Chin-Hwa, Ph.D.

Abraham Lincoln once said: "Let the people know the truth and the country will be safe." The Chinese Communist regime, however, not only strictly controls the media in mainland China by crushing freedom of speech and reporting of facts, its black hand of suppression has even extended into free societies. Without freedom, truth cannot be told, conscience and humanity will not exist and evil will be rampant. In fact, lack of freedom is the greatest misfortune in any society.

Let's start with an example in Taiwan:

I. Free media becomes the mouthpiece of propaganda

In August 2010, Taiwanese lawyers for Falun Gong practitioners brought unprecedented criminal charges against Huang Huahua, a former governor of Guangdong province, who was scheduled to lead a procurement delegation to Taiwan. Charges presented to the Taiwan High Prosecutors Office included the crime of genocide and violation of two UN treaties: The International Covenant on Civil and Political Rights and the International Covenant on Economic Social and Cultural Rights, both of which Taiwan adopted in 2009. The lawyers requested that his role in persecuting Falun Gong practitioners be investigated and that he be arrested while in Taiwan. Guangdong is one of the provinces in China where the persecution of Falun Gong is the most severe. The extent of cruelty is staggering, with a recent survey confirming 75 deaths and numerous injuries as a result of torture. Since Huang took the position as Party Secretary of Guangzhou, a city in Guangdong, he has been directly involved in commanding, plotting and organizing the persecution. One such example is that a Taiwanese Falun Gong practitioner was detained during his family visit in mainland China.

Taiwan has always claimed to be a nation "founded on human rights." Yet, three out of four major newspapers in Taiwan did not provide coverage on the charges brought against Huang and all major commercial television stations likewise did not give any report.

In fact, it is not uncommon for Taiwan media and even Western societies to neglect to report the brutal persecution of Falun Gong. Some even become the mouthpiece of the Chinese Communist Party (CCP) by spreading the Party's lies.

Why is the media not reporting the facts about Falun Gong? Why is the press no longer free in a free society? What means has Red China employed to force the media in a free society to succumb to its power? What impact does this have on society? Let's first discuss the issue of the CCP controlling the media in a free society.

II. Suppression of free media: Four methods employed by the CCP to control overseas media

1. Acquiring ownership and turning the media to its mouthpiece

Want Want Media Group in Taiwan is a good example. In 2008, *China Times*—one of the popular newspapers in Taiwan—was quickly declining due to fierce competition, rapid internet development and its own mismanagement. Tsai Eng Meng, a Taiwanese tycoon based in mainland China, purchased the company at an (unexpected) high price. Tsai was originally a businessman whose businesses conglomerates comprise *Want Want* snacks, beverages, real estate, insurance, financial services, management, hospitals, hotels, etc. More than 90 percent of his profit comes from the mainland Chinese market (*Legislature*, 2011). Forbes magazine recently listed him as the richest man in Taiwan and one of the richest in mainland China. However, according to a document in The *Economist* magazine published in April 2013, *Want Want* was listed as one of the largest enterprises funded by subsidies from the Chinese Government. According to the British magazine, the subsidy *Want Want* received from the CCP amounted to 11.3% of the company's net profit in 2011. We can see the close relationship between the CCP's support and *Want Want* Group's success.

A special report published in the February 2009 issue of Taiwan's *World Magazine* quoted a dialogue in a *Want Want* internal publication: "Reporting to the Director, we have bought up *China Times*." According to this article, Tsai spent NT$20.4 billion (around US$70 million) to acquire the *China Times* Corporations (including newspapers, a cable news channel and a wireless TV channel). He reported this to the director of the China-Taiwan Office (Wang Yi) one month after the transition. Tsai also said the media group has followed very well their "upper level's orders" to propagate the prosperity of the Motherland (i.e., mainland China). Wang Yi then replied: "If you have any need in the future, our office will certainly try our best to support you. (*Lin Xingfei*, 2009)

The above dialogue shows that *Want Want*, as a subsidized

corporation from China, has paid a high price to take over the media not simply for commercial purposes but also for a political purpose to serve both the interests of the government and the business. The academia refers to this relationship as "lackey" media. In fact, this happened not only in Taiwan, but also in Hong Kong and other countries. In recent years, overseas Chinese media ownership or equity have similarly been gradually bought up by these lackey businessmen. In free and democratic societies, the media emphasizes objectivity and neutrality, reporting the facts, serving the public interest and playing the role as the "fourth estate." However, these lackey media, although not directly under the CCP's control, act also as mouthpieces to serve the political interests of the CCP and report solely on "the prosperities of the Motherland."

2. Controlling news production, veering the course of news personnel, editorials and content

The second phase is to control the editorials and personnel. In February 2012, famed American Pulitzer prize winner Andrew Higgins, interviewed Tsai of the *Want Want* Group. He disclosed that *Want Want* media not only made major changes in its personnel but also controlled its editorial content in order to cater to the CCP. Higgins further revealed the similarities between Tsai's position and that of the CCP on the topics of the June 4th massacre and China's democracy. For example, Tsai said: "I realized that not that many people could really have died... [China] is very democratic in lots of places... [w]hether you like it or not, unification is going to happen sooner or later." Tsai claimed the reason to fire the chief editor of *China Times* was that she "hurt me by offending people, not just mainlanders. On lots of things, people were offended." Tsai added: Journalists are free to criticize, but they "need to think carefully before they write."[1]

Many Taiwanese intellectuals were very angry then. They launched waves of protests, criticizing his remarks against the facts known about the Tiananmen massacre in free societies. They also questioned the *Want Want* Group for purging dissenters, controlling personnel, and abusing freedom of the press. Also fired by the *Want Want* Media Group, the editor of the opinion page of *China Times* made a candid remark at a press conference that he was "not allowed to touch sensitive topics such as the June 4th Massacre, Falun Gong, the 1992 Consensus, and Dalai Lama, etc." Under such pressure, reporters fall into self-censorship: "Once they keep an inner police in mind, the editors will dodge sensitive issues by themselves." (*Xu Peijun*, 2012)

In fact, the lackey media does not only blatantly ignore the journalistic codes, but brazenly violate laws. At the beginning of this article, we mentioned that Huang Huahua led a procurement delegation to Taiwan in 2010, and was sued by Falun Gong lawyers. The majority of Taiwan's mainstream media, including *Want Want*, sidestepped this lawsuit. Instead, they all provided extensive news reports on Huang's "love" of Taiwan, how productive and fruitful his trip was; the speedy development of Guangdong Province, the golden opportunities for investment and the tight bond between Taiwan and "Motherland China." No attention was given to the Taiwanese businessmen's protests against him, Guangdong's severe environmental pollution, corruption and human rights violations. All the coverage turned out to be one-sided propaganda and advertisement. In fact, every piece of "positive news" was a paid advertisement. An investigation conducted by the Taiwan Board of Audit and Inspection in November 2011, confirmed that more than one medium practiced news placement, (i.e., "propaganda-disguised-as-news"). Such violations, the investigators argue, undermine journalistic professionalism, deceive readers, and threaten national security.

The CCP manipulates news media in many ways, including the acquisition of ownership, control of personnel, restriction of editorial autonomy and censorship of news coverage, etc., which have resulted in a total corruption of journalism. Reporters' consciences are suppressed and distorted and news content becomes mere propaganda and lies. The case of *Want Want* Group is just the tip of the iceberg.

3. Controlling of advertising and benefits, threatening and silencing the media

Even if there were no changes of the ownership structure, the CCP would still use economic incentives, advertisements and marketing benefits to manipulate the media. In fact, it has become common practice. For example, a highly popular TV talk show host, well-known for his outspoken style and sharp criticism against China, was replaced because of the pressure from the CCP. Hong Kong's *Apple Daily*, known for its pro-democracy and anti-communist stance, experienced significant advertising revocation from companies having business ties with China, resulting in a tremendous loss of revenue and 20% reduction in the number of newspaper pages. Another Hong Kong newspaper, *am730*, a free publication, which maintains a relatively mild position but has once criticized the CCP-installed Hong Kong government, had also suffered from advertising sources shut off by at least three Chinese banks, resulting in a serious blow to the newspaper's company.

As a matter of fact, the CCP's tactics of withdrawing advertisement from media has long existed, although it has become more pervasive, threatening all media intended to reach a Chinese-speaking audience. In order to survive, reporters have had to go against their conscience and silence their voice. It is truly unfortunate that the media in a free society would no longer be free.

4. Violent attacks to escalate fear

For those media or critics uncontrolled by CCP's various tactics in free societies, some frightening violence against dissidents in China has been obviously extended to overseas media. The first chapter of Hong Kong's Freedom Yearbook from 2014, "Violent Attacks on Reporters Endangers Freedom of the Press," points out that incidences of violent attacks on journalists in Hong Kong have risen drastically over the past two years and the seriousness of the violence has also been heightened, targeting not only outspoken reporters but also agency owners. The most tragic incident that occurred in the last few years was the former editor-in-chief of *Ming Pao*, Lau Chun-to (Liu Jintu), who was brutally stabbed in broad daylight, suffering severe injuries. The attack drew international attention and dozens of human rights organizations issued statements expressing their deep concern and condemn. They stated that the violence has affected not only the media, but challenges the rule of law in Hong Kong, and is a provocation against the Hong Kong press and freedom of speech in general.

In addition, incidents of violence against oppositional media in Hong Kong have been increasingly frequent in recent years: the gates to the residence of Lai Chi-ying (Li Zhiying), chairman of *Next Media* Ltd., the most anti-communist media group in Hong Kong, were crashed by an intruding car; tens of thousands of copies of the *Apple Daily* newspaper were maliciously set on fire in June 2013, Ming Pao once received a parcel of explosives; the sales stores of *Sing Tao Daily* and *Oriental Daily* News were damaged by criminals; executives of the Hong Kong *Morning Media* Group Limited were physically attacked in the business center of the town; the president of *iSunAffairs*.com magazine was attacked by two masked assailants with wooden sticks; the Epoch Times newspaper, established by Falun Gong practitioners, has been under constant assault. However, the vast majority of these violent attacks against media and their workers have remained unsolved.

In addition to these vicious, physical attacks, the CCP has reportedly built up a cyber army of hundreds of thousands of people to attack websites of large enterprises and government agencies, paralyzing websites or stealing internal intelligence and private information. Such high-tech crimes have escalated in recent years. For example, the night before a large parade for Hong Kong democracy and rights for public voting, the *Next Media*'s website was attacked at the so-called "national level," with up to forty million hits per second. Moreover, accompanied with internal data stealing, the hacking has threatened the security of individual and organizational information. The news websites set up by Falun Gong practitioners have been under constant attack for a long time. In response to China's cyber invasion and threats, many countries, including the USA, have heightened their security.

III. Conclusion: From repressing news to persecuting basic human rights

The CCP, through political, economic and editorial manipulation, let alone the threatening violence against media personnel, has exerted critical impacts on most media in free societies. For instance, the 2014, Freedom House Report ranked Hong Kong's press freedom as 74 among 197 countries, classified as a "partially free" country. In contrast, in 2002, Hong Kong was ranked 18th and well known as one of the freest countries in Asia. Ever since Hong Kong reverted back to Chinese rule in 1997, subjected to various CCP's manipulations through the years, Hong Kong has sadly slipped backwards from 18 to 74 in twelve years!

The freedom of the press in Taiwan, similarly influenced by the increasing "exchange programs between China and Taiwan," has, to some extent, declined as well every year. The 2014 Freedom of the Press Report released by Freedom House ranked Taiwan 47th, ahead of Hong Kong, and classified Taiwan as a "free country." However, in 2007 Taiwan was placed 32nd, and since then has declined by 15 places! The report suggested that the aforementioned acquisition of Taiwan's media by a Taiwanese-China tycoon has significantly impaired the press freedom in Taiwan.

Professor Yu Ying-shih (Yu Yingshi), the well-known Chinese historian and an elected Fellow of Academia Sinica of Taiwan, published a letter in 2012, pointing out that "in Taiwan, a number of powerful politicians and wealthy businessmen were determined to pander to the wishes of the CCP under motives of absolute self-interests. They have infiltrated every nook and cranny in Taiwan, and buying up public media is just one part of it." He openly questioned the negative impact of the CCP's control of public opinion by purchasing and merging of Taiwan media from 2012 to 2013.

From examples cited in this article, one can observe the CCP's totalitarian control of freedom and conscience inside China as well as overseas. It has severely eroded the core values of journalism in free societies, including truthful reporting of facts, monitoring power, and safeguarding public interest. People rely on unbiased news coverage to get information on every aspect of life, from personal safety and health to civil and political rights. People make choices depending on true and complete information through free-flowing conduits and diverse opinions. This free flow of information is the basis for the healthy operation of a democratic society, where power could be supervised, the abuse of power can be exposed, the interests of the people can be safeguarded and a sound political system could be entrenched. Truthful information is also critical in maintaining the order and peace of the international community. At present, the international community is calling the CCP out on a number of offenses, including manipulating exchange rates, expanding its military, practicing exploitative colonial diplomacy, plundering mineral resources, copyright violations, exporting products made by slave labor, suffusing global markets with toxic food and toys, etc.

Countless children died under the collapsed school buildings during the 2008 Wenchuan earthquake in Sichuan Province as a result of shoddy construction. Numerous babies suffered from severe health problems while many died after consuming poisonous infant formulas intentionally tainted for increasing profits. China's land, air, water and farms are ruthlessly contaminated, impacting both domestic and exported products. Many countries have paid a high price for the CCP's misdeeds while countless people have been hurt and even lost their lives. Yet, under the CCP's blockade of information and sugarcoated propaganda, corrective measures could not be addressed, and most Chinese citizens are even not aware of the problems.

The Communist China 's cruel abuse of power has led to the persecution of Falun Gong practitioners, people of different faiths and creeds and all kinds of dissidents. What is even more despicable is the loss of conscience and medical ethics that have resulted in forced organ harvesting, selling organs for profit and promptly cremating bodies—dead or alive—to cover up any trace of these crimes. Behind all sorts of evil and violence is the autocratic regime's systemic abuse of power, corrupt officials, social injustice, and media control. The problems are numerous, but the facts are blocked from public access. As a result, parents are incapable of protecting their children, teachers are incapable of protecting students, citizens are incapable of safeguarding the environment and there is no social stability to allow for the survival and welfare of the next generation. The CCP uses its mouthpiece—the state media—to praise the Party as being

"Grand, Glorious, and Righteous" to brainwash its people. Those without access to external information echo the Party's propaganda and become accomplices to those who slander the innocent and violate human rights.

The deeper problem of the CCP's totalitarian regime is the threat they pose to individual well-being, so that protection and satisfaction of one's own needs overshadows the needs of others. When survival is threatened, people choose to abandon their conscience and succumb to evil, some even voluntarily become accomplices of violence. One of the main themes at the United States Holocaust Museum in Washington, DC is that the ones closest to the victims often become their aggressors: "Some [perpetrators] were neighbors." Under the lies and threats of violence, good friends, good neighbors, or good classmates become accomplices of persecution, transforming from angels to demons. Therefore, it is not only the violation of professional journalism, but also the most evil distortion of human nature that we are witnessing today from the CCP's control of the media.

The human rights issue of Falun Gong is a good example. Under the CCP's threats, the media either cooperate with the CCP-controlled official media or remain silent. Even when encountered with the aforementioned unprecedented accusation against the China governor, most of the mainstream media chose to remain silent. What is even more pitiable, some media actually portrayed a blatantly corrupted official as a "good governor who cares deeply about the people!" It becomes difficult for the general public to distinguish facts from lies. As a result, they may become the persecutor's advocates. Journalists who choose to lie have not only betrayed their professional conscience, but also become the persecutor's accomplices. When there is no truth and freedom, one cannot judge with conscience. Therefore, by controlling and suppressing news, China's authoritarian regime is not simply victimizing the targeted group, but all people.

Although the so-called "China factor," through the exchange of various interests, has eroded the foundation of journalism and democratic societies, there are still some people who try to know the facts and then understand the truth. Because these people cherish freedom and maintain conscience, they rise to expose and resist the suppression. An example is the social movement against the merger and acquisition of *China Times* media group by *Want Want* Corporation. More than ten thousands of people, including teachers and students in academia, as well as NGOs and community groups joined forces together. Through the internet, they formed a momentous movement calling for freedom of the press, diversity and media reform. When a large number of citizens spontaneously protested on the streets, the Taiwan government was finally propelled to pay more attention to the regulation on media diversity and merger review. In addition to setting strict conditions regulating the merger by the NCC (National Communications Committee), the Legislative Yuan also launched actions of revising the anti-monopoly media law. Finally, under the pressure of tremendous civil opposition, *Want Want* media group backed off from additional mergers. This is truly the power of goodness that won a victory for civil liberties.

Falun Gong practitioners have been one of the most active groups in the world helping people to see beyond the CCP's propaganda. For over 15 years, practitioners in and outside of China—often at great risk to their lives—have continued to dedicate their time, effort and resources to reveal the facts not only of the persecution of Falun Gong but also of the various abuses by the CCP. Through passing out truth-clarification flyers and other materials on the street, visiting Congressional and Senate offices, working with the courts and speaking to the media, Falun Gong practitioners enable people to learn the facts and understand the truth. Through their activities to rescue persecuted practitioners in China and stand up against the illegal and immoral persecution, Falun Gong practitioners empower people in becoming courageous enough to not only step up to support Falun Gong, but also take initiative themselves to help end the persecution; and in doing so, they change themselves and change the world.

The famous reporter and political commentator Walter Lippmann once said, "Without facts, there can be no liberty."[2] No matter how authoritarian regimes try to suppress freedom and truth, and how much the media has been controlled and threatened, it's really simple to fight such evil. If everyone of us takes some effort to understand the truth from the materials distributed by Falun Gong practitioners, then the truth will no longer be blocked and the power of facts and righteousness will expand, then the evil and its lies will lose its supporting roots and collapse.

---

[1] Higgins, Andrew. Tycoon prods Taiwan closer to China. The Washington Post. (2012.01.21).

[2] Walter Lippmann, Liberty and News. 1920. https://archive.org/details/libertyandnews01lippgoog

Section II

POLITICS, SOCIETY, ECONOMICS

Falun Gong is not a Cult

By David Kilgour, J.D.

Eight years ago, David Matas and I, as volunteers joined the international campaign to raise awareness about organ pillaging/trafficking from Falun Gong practitioners in China. The persecution began in mid-1999, but we as independent investigators could find no evidence of commerce in organs seized from Falun Gong before 2001. The revised Matas-Kilgour report is available in almost 20 languages on the Web (See www.david-kilgour.com or www.organharvestinvestigation.net).

On one occasion, our delegation arrived at a national parliament in central Europe, expecting to meet with a multi-party group of legislators, only to find that the local MP entrusted to invite others, had at the last moment decided not to do so. His stated rationale was that his caucus is faith-based and that Falun Gong is a different religion from his own.

In none of the approximately 50 countries Matas and I have now visited separately or together on this issue since our report came out in 2006, have we heard a Falun Gong practitioner speak other than positively about other spiritual communities. Which religion, moreover, does not identify with Falun Gong's core principles of "truth, compassion and forbearance"? The serenity and non-violence its practitioners have demonstrated seemingly without exception in the face of myriad beatings, imprisonments, torture and murder across China since mid-1999 are impressive to anyone aware of the details.

The twentieth century was no doubt the worst in recorded history for the brutality directed at faith communities by governments. One probably high estimate of the number of individuals of all nationalities who died prematurely for their faiths between 1900 and 2000, is a staggering 169 million, including 70 million Muslims, 35 million Christians, 11 million Hindus, nine million Jews, four million Buddhists, two million Sikhs and one million Baha'is.

Many died from inter- or intra-faith violence, but most perished at the hands of totalitarian regimes, which loathed all religions, largely because the deeper loyalties of their members lay elsewhere than with local or national despots. Mao, Stalin, Hitler, Poll Pot and others, who committed a vast range of what we now term crimes against humanity, murdered untold tens of millions of their fellow citizens for having a spiritual faith. The hostile attitude towards all religion in totalitarian Beijing is the first major reason for the persecution Falun Gong practitioners have faced across China up to and including the present time.

Clive Ansley of British Columbia, who practiced law in Shanghai for 13 years and is the North American chair of the Coalition to investigate the persecution of Falun Gong, recently noted:

> But there are from 100,000 to 200,000 Falun Gong practitioners who have been murdered on the operating tables of China. And had their organs stolen and sold for profit. And there is hardly a murmur about this anywhere. We have seen a stream of reports in the newspapers, in all the media, about Darfur, Burma and Tibet. Mia Farrow protested what she called the "Genocide Olympics" because of the indirect genocide China carried out in Darfur; yet she never once mentioned the direct genocide the Chinese Communist Party has been systematically implementing on a daily basis since 1999. I never see a reference to the genocide against Falun Gong in any of these discussions about Chinese

atrocities in Darfur or Tibet.

The media systematically ignores the most bestial atrocity that the world has seen since the Holocaust. Over the last 15 years the most barbaric Crime Against Humanity in modern history has been unfolding daily in China and it has provoked an absolutely thunderous silence on the part of our media and most of our North American politicians. This is the Holocaust all over again, but with a new and appalling dimension.

The second reason was its immensely popular appeal across China after being introduced by founder Master Li Hongzhi to the general public in rural China only, in 1992. The phenomenal growth was partly because of its deep roots in Daoism, Confucianism, Buddhism and other prominent features of indigenous Chinese culture, physical exercises and spirituality. These traditional prominent features of Chinese culture had been suppressed by Mao from 1949 until his death in 1976. By 1999, there were, by the party-state's own estimates, more than 70 million Falun Gong practitioners across China—more than the membership of the Chinese Communist party.

A related negative factor for Jiang and other Party officials was Falun Gong's lack of hierarchy and structure, which made it impossible for them to control its membership and activities.

These factors help explain why Jiang Zemin, as party-state boss in 1999 and probably earlier, developed his irrational hatred for Falun Gong.

Cult?

Jiang's 'Biggest Untruth', i.e., that Falun Gong is an "evil cult", is reminiscent of messages the government of Rwanda broadcast through its party media against the Tutsi minority before the genocide committed across that country between April and June of 1994. The Bolsheviks in Russia took a similar path against their own prescribed list of party enemies after the Communist Revolution of 1917. Hitler's Nazis used it against various minority communities, especially German Jews, after 1933.

There was such a continuous toxic stream of propaganda against Falun Gong in party-state-controlled media across China after 1999 that many Chinese nationals and persons outside the country naively accepted party-state lies on this and other matters.

Ian Johnson, a former Beijing bureau chief for the *Wall Street* Journal, who won a Pulitzer Prize for his reporting on Falun Gong, has lifted a number of curtains on the party-state persecution of Falun Gong in his 2005 book *Wild Grass*:

- Declaring Falun Gong a cult was one of the regime's "most brilliant moves" because it put Falun Gong on the defensive to prove its innocence and "cloaked the government's crackdown with the legitimacy of the West's anti-cult movement. The government quickly picked up the vocabulary of the anti-cult movement, launching Web sites and putting forth overnight experts, who intoned that Master Li was no different from Jim Jones, the head of the Peoples Temple who in 1978 allegedly killed 912 members, or the Church of Scientology, whose members are allegedly brainwashed into giving huge amounts of money."

- "To prove its point, the government came up with a series of lurid stories about people who had cut open their stomachs looking for the Dharma Wheel that was supposed to spin inside it. Others were presented, whose relatives had died after performing Falun Gong exercises instead of taking medicine..."

- The problem was that few of these arguments held up. The government never allowed victims of Falun Gong to be interviewed independently, making it almost impossible to verify their claims. And even if one took all the claims at face value, they made up a very small percentage of Falun Gong's total number of adherents..."

- "More fundamentally, the group didn't meet many common definitions of a cult: its members marry outside the group, have outside friends, hold normal jobs, do not live isolated from society, do not believe the world's end is imminent and do not give significant amounts of money to the organization. Most important, suicide is not accepted, nor is physical violence..."

As a former Crown counsel, I spoke about the dangers of cults and some new religious movements at an international conference at the University of Alberta in 2004 (June 11), the text of which is available on my website (david-kilgour.com/mp/cultsandnewreligions.htm).

At the same conference, held in Lister Hall, a student residence at the University of Alberta in Edmonton and two staff members from the consulate of China in Calgary were distributing pamphlets, which attacked Falun Gong, contrary to the 'inciting hatred' against an identifiable religious or cultural community section of Canada's Criminal Code. Two Edmonton city police officers concluded on the basis of the pamphlet contents that the 'diplomats' should be charged, but the provincial Attorney General of the day refused to give the required consent to going ahead with charges. There were diplomatic immunity issues, but in my judgment at the time, he should have consented. There are more details of the incident in section 21 of our report ('Incitement to Hatred') and the police report of the incident is exhibit 30.

Professor David Ownby of the University of Montreal, who did specific research on Falun Gong and is cited in our report, concluded:

- Falun Gong practitioners in North America are well-educated and tend to live in nuclear families. Many work with computers or in finance; some are engineers.

- Falun Gong Practitioners do not have financial obligations to their faith community; as well, they do not live in isolation and are law-abiding.

- Falun Gong is not a cult

Ownby's conclusion accords with that of many independent observers, including David Matas and myself. In the now 115 or so countries where Falun Gong exists, there is only one, China (and possibly Vladimir Putin's Russia), where its practitioners appear not to be considered good citizens and exemplary members of their respective civil societies.

Liberty Indivisible

One researcher on the persecution of religions in China suggested several years ago that there were then probably as many Christians attending services across China each week–mostly in secret—as were doing so openly across Europe. In standing up for the principles of the United Nations Universal Human Rights Declaration for a young spiritual community like Falun Gong, the short-sighted MP mentioned above would ultimately be defending freedom of religion generally in China. The constitution of China says its citizens "enjoy freedom of religious belief" (art. 36), although those beyond the so-called "patriotic churches" are often denied the right to practice their faiths.

China's party-state considers all spiritual communities to be deviations in accord with the dialectic materialism of Karl Marx. Enter, for example, "Chinese government persecution of Christians" on Google.ca and fully 1, 970,000 entries today are listed, many of them appalling. Replace "Christians" with a number of other groups and you get:

- foreigners-14,800,000 entries

- Muslims-3,180,000

- democrats-43,400,000

- women-6,440,,000

- Falun Gong-290,000

- Tibetans- 441,000

- Gays and lesbians—1,660,000

- Uyghurs—4,210,000

- Journalists—approx. 37,000,000

- Lawyers—2,820,000

- Investors—32,600,000

- Foreign investors—39,200,000

- Entrepreneurs—61,000,000

Most Falun Gong prisoners of conscience are in forced labor camps in appalling conditions, making a wide range of products for export, including Christmas decorations, in violation of

World Trade Organization (WTO) rules.

Google "Chinese government corruption" and you can access 36,900,000 items. "Chinese government secret executions" brings 8,460,000. Another item that caught my eye was "Chinese Government denies", which has 4,140,000 entries. The Beijing party-state specializes in false denials, including such matters as whether there was a 2003 SARS epidemic in China, whether anyone died at Tiananmen Square in June 1989, and whether it pillages/traffics in the organs of Falun Gong.

Conclusion

Human dignity today is indivisible around the world. All faith communities and other members of civil societies everywhere should be fully united on issues like the ones Falun Gong practitioners have faced daily for too long across China. If the peoples in open societies around the world don't unite on such matters, some of the world's remaining dictatorships will only repeat the terrible ravages of the last century.

As indicated above, one issue is clear beyond doubt: Falun Gong, whose practitioners prefer to be termed an exercise group with meditation, rather than a religion, is not a cult.

Falun Gong's Influence on China's Politics

By Yuan Hong Bing

1. Falun Gong does not subjectively engage in politics

Turning a blind eye to the Chinese Communist Party (CCP) tyranny's persecution against Falun Gong, some Chinese intellectuals at home and abroad who think highly of themselves have remained silent to this day. When defending their own silence, a favorite rhetoric is: "we do not participate in politics"; "we are impartial to both the Communist Party and Falun Gong, because they are both engaged in politics."

The Chinese Embassy in Australia once issued a statement denouncing the *Nine Commentaries on the Communist Party* as "anti-Chinese articles" and alleging that Falun Gong was an "anti-Chinese political reactionary organization". However, this allegation is an insult to the truth.

From the "Politics in Command" theory of the Mao Zedong's era to the "Emphasis on Politics" movement of Jiang Zemin's time, they have consistently used state terrorism to indoctrinate the Chinese people that engaging in politics is a prerogative of the Communist Party. The history of the Communist Party has consistently demonstrated to the people that politics involves waves after waves of ideological purge and political persecutions, which desecrate humanity, destroy culture, slaughter innocent lives, poison the collective conscience, and deprive human rights. The Communist Party has transformed politics into an arena of bloodiness, conspiracies and barbarism. Politics has become evil itself. In this sense, the general Chinese public, including Falun Gong practitioners, have been deprived of the right to "engage in politics". Just as being political is the prerogative of the Communist Party, so is being evil.

Since July 1999, Jiang Zemin and the Communist Party's band of bureaucrats used political and social resources they seized through tyranny to launch a bloody and colossal political persecution to exterminate the faith of Falun Gong. Jiang Zemin's crimes of genocide and the extermination of faith have angered both heaven and humankind. The viciousness of these crimes was only matched by the deeds of a handful of dictators such as Mao Zedong, Adolf Hitler, Joseph Stalin, Pol Pot, and Deng Xiaoping.

Faced with political persecution like tsunamis and earthquakes in scale and ferocity, against shameless slander, arrests, torture, and murder, Falun Gong practitioners upheld their belief with iron resilience and steadfastness. Their peaceful resistance against this reign of terror is testament that faith can overcome tyranny. In their continuous efforts to expose the evils of CCP's regime to the world, they are sowing the seeds of freedom of belief.

In recent years, Falun Gong's statements and actions has demonstrated that they are not only safeguarding their own right to freedom of belief, but also pursuing the basic human rights for those other groups that are persecuted by state terror. History has recorded that in the latter years of the so-called Jiang Zemin era, Falun Gong practitioners became the main pillar that upheld and defended human rights in China. Perhaps history will remember a lot more.

The CCP bureaucrats denounce Falun Gong practitioners' peaceful resistance and preservation of human rights as "engaging in politics". Please answer this: Does "not engaging in politics" mean turning a blind eye and a deaf ear to Jiang Zemin's crimes of genocide and extermination of faith? Does "not engaging in politics" mean surrendering without a whimper when the CCP trampled over human rights and abused the people? Does "not engaging in politics" really mean daring not to speak the truth against lies fabricated by the CCP propaganda machine to cover up their crimes? Do the Chinese people really need to act like masochists and slaves and silently accept the CCP's oppression and abuses in order to escape the accusation of "engaging in politics"?

The laws of the Heaven are clear! The laws of the Heaven are just! Is there a need to say out loud what is right and wrong?

Falun Gong is not a political organization. It is a cultivation practice. Falun Gong has not engaged in politics. This is because, to this day, Falun Gong practitioners' beliefs and actions have clearly shown: they have no interest in state power; they are simply informing humankind of the evils of the CCP regime. They have no interest in state power; they are simply looking for a space that will allow them the freedom to believe.

Some self-righteous intellectuals claim: "We do not engage in politics. Between the CCP and Falun Gong, we do not support or oppose either of them." When I hear such statements I always feel deeply mortified and ashamed. I'm ashamed of how far the intellectuals have fallen. Such statements are hypocritical. Hidden underneath the hypocrisy are their cowardice, servility, selfishness and lack of courage and righteous spirit to advocate for justice. I want to ask these sanctimonious intellectuals: if you witness a band of thugs brutally abuse the weak and innocent, would you still claim: "we do not support or oppose either of them, because we are impartial"?

At this point, I would like to say to those scholars who do not agree with the beliefs of Falun Gong: let's reflect on those timeless words of Voltaire – "I don't agree with you what you say, but I'll defend to the death your right to say it." If we put these words into action, we will be respected in history. Please do not forget – when we enter into old age, our children and grandchildren may look into our eyes and ask: "During that brutal and colossal political persecution, what did you do? Did you shamefully remain silent?"

The Chinese Embassy labeled the *Nine Commentaries on the Communist Party* as "anti-Chinese articles" and Falun Gong as an "anti-Chinese organization". The Communist Party equates itself to the Chinese people, which is utterly shameless. No single political organization can compare itself to the Chinese people who are the inheritor of 5,000 years of civilization. For the betrayals and mutilations they have committed against the Chinese people, the CCP should eternally kneel in front of the headstones of the Chinese ancestors to repent for its crimes.

After they betrayed the spirit of Chinese culture to Marxism, a German's theory built on hatred and violence; after their stupidity and cruelty starved tens of millions of peasants to death; after they persecuted and murdered millions of intellectuals; after they slaughtered millions of Tibetans who stood firmly by their beliefs; after they instigated Pol Pot to kill millions of Cambodian people—including countless ethnic Chinese; after they impoverished hundreds of millions of peasants as third-class citizens for over half a century; after they drove tens of millions of unemployed and migrant workers into poverty; after they brought about endless social tragedies and human disasters; after they bred a class of corrupted and degenerated officials unmatched in history; after they surrendered the society's wealth to an alliance of corrupted powers and organized crimes; after all this and having injured the Chinese people so grievously, the Communist Party still dares to equate itself to the Chinese people, are they not utterly shameless?

History and truth have prevailed over propaganda and lies. It is clear that the Communist Party, particularly its band of bureaucrats, are the disgrace of China, the criminals against the Chinese nation and the source of all evil.

Courageously exposing the CCP's evil crimes is the deepest and most sincere love for the Chinese nation. Only by putting an end to the CCP's tyrannical rule can the Chinese people be truly saved. Bury the CCP tyranny and wash away a century of humiliation suffered by China.

A millennium may pass by with ease, but the sins of the CCP will not be erased.

2. Falun Gong movement's objective impact on Chinese politics

Subjectively speaking, Falun Gong has no desire to engage in politics. However, objectively the resistance to persecution by the spiritual practitioners of Falun Gong has had a profound effect on Chinese politics, which has mainly manifested in the following aspects:

(1) It has become one of the factors to lead Chinese history out of the shadow of the CCP's state terrorism.

(2) The most important vehicle for the CCP to maintain its totalitarian rule is state violence, which causes widespread fear among the people, and in turn, destroys the people's will to defy its control. In 1989, the CCP regime unleashed hundreds of thousands of troops and left Beijing in a bloodbath, executed the horrific "Tiananmen Square Massacre". Then CCP leader Deng Xiaoping and his 'political elites' even threatened to "kill 200,000 people to ensure stability for 20 years". It shrouded China in a bloody atmosphere of state terrorism.

After the Tiananmen Square Massacre, there were attempts by Beijing's liberal intellectuals to break through the state terror. Such attempts included the "Tidal Wave of the History", the Olympic Hotel Anti-leftist Conference of over a hundred Liberal Intellectuals, establishing the "Labor Rights Protection Alliance," collecting signature petitions to "Support Freedom Painter Yan Zhengxue under Police Persecution". Despite the above, the majority of the people were living in fear after the massacre in Beijing.

On April 25, 1999, to protest against defamation of Falun Gong by the CCP propaganda machine and an academic closely linked to Jiang Zemin, over ten thousand Falun Gong practitioners went to Beijing to appeal. They peacefully practiced meditation around the CCP's Central Government compound Zhongnanhai, and showed devotion to their belief in "Truth, Compassion and Tolerance". This large scale protest by the spiritual practitioners of Falun Gong demonstrated courage and valor powered by faith, which far outshone CCP's iron fist. It shattered the dark fear that had oppressed the Chinese people since the Tiananmen Square Massacre. From then on, public uprisings to "safeguard human rights and fight against tyranny" spreading like wild fire across the East Asian continent. Today, they are numbered in the hundreds of thousands each year in China.

The above facts have shown that in their resistance against persecution, the spiritual practitioners of Falun Gong have been instrumental—in fact they deserve the highest honor for it, in leading the Chinese nation out of the widespread terror since the Tiananmen Square Massacre and into an era of prevalent protests against the tyranny.

(3) Falun Gong's efforts to oppose the persecution and clarify the truth have exposed the evil nature of CCP's totalitarian rule, quickened the political awakening of Chinese public.

After the Tiananmen Square Massacre, the CCP relied on its mouthpieces to cover up its unforgivable crimes against humanity, deceive the international community and consolidate its autocratic control. Their puppets included scholars they had trained and pampered, writers directly associated with the ruling class, as well as some international "sinologists" and "China experts" on their payroll. From all sorts of angles, they fabricated a series of lies about CCP's upcoming political reforms and spread the delusion that "economic reforms" will lead to China's democratization. These lies and delusions, to a great extent, hindered the Chinese people's resolve to rise up and battle against the CCP's tyranny. In addition, a class of pseudo-liberal intellectuals such as Liu Xiaobo followed the American and European appeasement politicians, promoted the idea of compromising with the CCP and claimed that both the CCP's autocratic system and China's human rights situations were gradually improving. This also greatly aided the CCP in camouflaging its evil nature.

Under such a complex background, Falun Gong's spiritual practitioners sustained their anti-persecution and truth clarification activities, day in and day out for over a decade. They thoroughly and effectively exposed the CCP's evil nature, which repudiates history, humankind, society, human nature and the Chinese culture. Like the grand Chinese music of ancient times, the truth came out thundering and awakening. Falun Gong practitioners' campaigns allowed more and more Chinese people to realize that "only without the CCP, there will be a new China". This is a great political awakening, and it has laid the essential ideological foundation for a democratic revolution in contemporary China.

(4) Falun Gong practitioners initiated a modern day spiritual uprising amongst the Chinese people – quitting their memberships from the CCP and its affiliated organizations.

The CCP regime is a group of criminals who have perpetrated innumerable crimes against humanity against people of various ethnic origins across the East Asian continent. It is the most shameless and the largest group of corrupt officials in human history. It is a political mafia that controls its people through secret police and surveillance. By using the Communist Party culture from the West, the CCP destroyed the Chinese people's civilized homeland and spiritual birthplace. They are China's most vicious traitor throughout its millennia of history.

From the history of the CCP's reign over the East Asian continent, we can draw the following conclusions: the CCP tyranny is the source of all evil; contemporary Chinese people are the political slaves under the Marxist control and have lost their cultural roots; a "Chinese Dream" that truly belongs to the people would be toabolish the CCP regime and create a free and democratic federal China.

The ever growing movement to quit the CCP and its affiliated organizations, initiated by spiritual practitioners of Falun Gong practitioners, is disintegrating the CCP at its foundation. Spreading like wild fire, it is capturing the hearts of the public. In truth, quitting the CCP is Chinese people's way to liberate themselves from the ideological shackles. It is a monumental uprising in the spiritual realm and will ultimately manifest into political changes that will alter the course of history.

3. Conclusion

Subjectively, Falun Gong does not engage in politics, but objectively it has had a political impact on advancing China's democratization. One may say its outcome is serendipitous.

In its colossal persecution against Falun Gong, the CCP regime rapidly evolved into the darkest form of despotism, namely, political mafia dominated by spies and secret police.

After the CCP's 18th Congress, Mao Zedong's "Old Red Guards" (the equivalent of the SS Corps of Nazi Party), a group of anti-human criminals, had full control of CCP's powers. Consequently, China entered into its darkest period in its millennia of history. However, as the CCP's tyranny evolved into its most vile and cruel form, it also heralded the demise of its anti-human and anti-social reign. "A new China without the CCP", a "Chinese Dream" that belongs to the people will inevitably become a magnificent reality.

Pouring the Entire Nation's Efforts into Persecution

By Zhang Tianliang, Ph.D.

On July 29, 2014, Xinhua News Agency, the propaganda outlet of the Chinese Communist Party (CCP), published a news brief that would inevitably capture the world's attention: Zhou Yongkang, former member of the Politburo Standing Committee and Secretary of the Central Politics and Law Committee, was under investigation for alleged serious discipline violations. Zhou is the most senior official being investigated on corruption charges since the CCP established its regime 60 years ago.

In fact, the accusation of "corruption" was just the cover story. The real reason is Zhou Yongkang, Bo Xilai, and others, under the support of Jiang Zemin and Zeng Qinghong, had planned a coup to overthrow President Xi Jinping[1] and replace him with Bo Xilai. Therefore, Xi Jinping had no choice but to remove Zhou, Bo and even their behind-the-scenes supporters.

The actual reason for the coup stems from the fact that more than a decade ago, Jiang and his faction had poured the entire nation's resources to suppress Falun Gong, resulting in an earth-shattering blood debt. The only way to avoid the inevitable exposure is to tightly grasp onto power and to continue the policy of persecution; Bo Xilai was the hand-picked candidate to achieve this task.

After the CCP established its regime, the persecution suffered by the military personnel of the Chinese Nationalist Party, members of various religious and civil organizations, rural and urban property owners, as well as the targeted victims of the decade long "Cultural Revolution," it caused the Chinese people to be vulnerable to the CCP's capability for brutality. Similarly the "June 4th Incident," otherwise known as the "Tiananmen Square Massacre," in the eyes of the world, showcased the CCP's determination of its persecutory tactics. Faced with Falun Gong's widespread and sustained nonviolent resistance, one can therefore insinuate from the historical context the extent of how cruel and intense the CCP's persecution could be.

The former CCP General Secretary Jiang Zemin changed Deng Xiaoping's motto of "all resources and efforts are centered on economic development" to "all resources and efforts are centered on suppressing Falun Gong," and transformed the structure of the national authorities to implement such a policy. This article will examine the gravity of the persecution of Falun Gong from this perspective.

I. The first persistent, large scale, non-violent resistance in CCP history

In the history of the Communist Party, it has never taken more than three days to completely suppress a certain group or individual. Therefore, Jiang was convinced that it would only take him no more than three months to eradicate Falun Gong. However, he was met with Falun Gong's enduring peaceful resistance. This resistance has three key characteristics: endurance, large scale and non-violence.

The CCP's persecution has persisted for over 15 years now. From the onset, Falun Gong practitioners in mainland China publicly posted flyers, distributed CD's, hung banners, circulated the *Nine Commentaries on the Communist Party*, and experienced imprisonment and torture at the hands of the CCP. Yet irrespective of the punishment, they maintained their endurance on a large scale. Falun Gong practitioners overseas have established and managed a variety of media platforms, engaged in litigation action against Communist leaders responsible for the persecution, broke through the CCP's internet blockades, revived traditional Chinese culture, as well as showcased classical Chinese dance in the annual Shen Yun performances. These activities have gained momentum in the last 15 years, going from strength to strength.

II. From "all resources and efforts are centered on economic development" to "all resources and efforts are centered on suppressing Falun Gong"

(1) A considerable financial investment

Nevertheless, the cost of the CCP's persecution of Falun Gong is also considerable. What may cost Falun Gong practitioners one US dollar or one minute's worth of time, the CCP may have to invest thousands or tens of thousands of US dollars and a few days or months' to counteract. To give the simplest example: when Falun Gong practitioners' overseas software developers performed an upgrade to break the internet blockade, the response from the CCP resulted in an immense investment in research and development. Thousands or tens of thousands of firewall upgrades occurred, and export bandwidth at a rate of more than two Tbps data (one trillion bits per second) had to be filtered.[23] For instance, when Falun Gong practitioners filed one lawsuit against Jiang Zemin, the CCP would send a large special interest group to lobby the State Council, the Ministry of Justice, the courts and all relevant personnel, and would make great concessions on trade in order to evade further detailed investigation on Jiang Zemin.

A survey showed that the CCP spends a quarter of its gross domestic product (GDP) on the persecution of Falun Gong practitioners. The amount of resources utilized to fund the persecution is equivalent to the means of subsidizing a war. [4]

(2) The heavy price of persecution

Jiang Zemin changed Deng Xiaoping's "all resources and efforts are centered on economic development" to "all resources and efforts are centered on suppressing Falun Gong." From both domestic and foreign affairs, one can already gain some insight.

In terms of internal political affairs, the CCP had no choice but to adjust its organizational structure and set up the unlawful "610 Office" to suppress Falun Gong, which monopolizes the entire public security, procuratorial, legislative, and judiciary sectors, but also the domains of intelligence, diplomatic affairs, finance, the military, armed police, medical institutions and mass communications, etc.[5] The CCP claims that the superiority of socialism is its "concentrating power in doing great work." The "610 Office" is such an agency that can virtually mobilize all national resources through the channels of the major institutions. It is in summary, another central authority outside of the Politburo Standing Committee. This central authority is headed by Li Lanqing, the former First Deputy Prime Minister of the State Council and Jiang's close friend. Luo Gan assumed a specific authority of command and supervision while the central power is directly controlled by Jiang.

Because of Falun Gong's resolute and uncompromising

resilience, Jiang Zemin's frustration and humiliation escalated the persecution relentlessly, this exacerbated the already existing bloodbath. In 2002, before the 16th National Congress, Jiang made his last international official visit to Chicago, where he was served a legal summons and complaint about human rights violations against Falun Gong practitioners.

On the one hand, due to the litigation instigated by Falun Gong practitioners, there is the possibility of repercussions for Jiang's reign of terror. On the other hand, the majority of members of the Politburo Standing Committee did not have any vested interest in the persecution. In order to ensure his power would remain intact, Jiang Zemin enforced a fundamental change in the Politburo Standing Committee before the end of term as General Secretary. Jiang strategically placed two of his henchmen as the eighth and ninth members to the original seven member committee. Li Changchun was in charge of anti-Falun Gong propaganda and Luo Gan was responsible for ensuring the continued violent persecution against Falun Gong practitioners.

Jiang also re-branded the CCP's traditional title of "core leadership" and replaced it with a new title of "collective leadership." This act deliberately and effectively stripped his successor, Hu Jintao, the authority over Li Changchun, Luo Gan and their corresponding political portfolios.

The CCP morphed from a dictatorship to an "oligarchy" system, with a pool of nine Standing Committee members, whereby each position had specific and independent responsibilities. This resulted in: 1) Luo Gan as a member of the Politburo Standing Committee having an instrumental role which gave him access to mobilize the country's resources to continue Jiang's repressive policies. 2) The autonomous roles of nine committee members meant that Luo Gan's authority was not scrutinized or challenged. This important organizational restructure was orchestrated by

Jiang, with the primary aim to target the persecution of Falun Gong practitioners.

Meanwhile, Jiang also made a decision that shocked the international community. Jiang organized Zhang Wannian to employ a paramilitary coup, in order for a special motion to re-elect Jiang Chairman of the Central Military Commission for an extended term after the 2002 16th National Congress. Jiang was prepared to concentrate another two more years to resolve the Falun Gong issue. However in 2004, when the persecution became increasingly difficult to sustain, Jiang had no choice but to withdraw from the CCP's highest position of power.

On the diplomatic front and on the surface, the CCP places Taiwan, Tibet, and pro-democracy issues in centerpiece positions, when in fact, the Falun Gong issue is its core interest. For example, the "Washington Times" reported in March 9, 2001, that Zhu Qizhen and Li Daoyu, former Chinese Ambassadors to the U.S., and Zhang Wenpu, former Chinese Ambassador to Canada, met with former United States National Security Adviser Condoleezza Rice. During the meeting, without forewarning, one of the former Ambassadors pulled out a prepared speech and proceeded to read from the paper that focused on how Falun Gong was posing a threat to the Chinese government. Rice was reportedly "angered by the Chinese diplomats' tirade and quickly ended the meeting after the 20-minute reading." [6]

(3) The failed assassination plots and coup d'état

At a banquet, Liu Jing, former deputy director of the "610 Office," revealed that the CCP leadership was divided into two factions over the Falun Gong issue. Hu Jintao's disagreement with the suppression of Falun Gong was met with reprimand and vehement opposition by Jiang Zemin, who subsequently attempted to plot Hu's assassination.[7]

On November 15, 2006, Hong Kong "Trends" magazine reported the year's exclusive "May 1st incident," where Hu Jintao was almost assassinated in the Yellow Sea. An investigation found that the orders for the assassination originated from Jiang himself. Admiral Zhang Dingfa was designated to execute Jiang's attempted assassination mission to kill Hu. At the end of 2006, Zhang's death was announced. There was no mourning and no eulogy. Both the official "Xinhua News Agency" and the "Liberation Army Daily" were silent on the issue. Only the "People's Navy News" published a brief article. [8]

During the 17th National Congress in 2007, because of Hu's interference, Jiang failed to have Bo Xilai, his favorite loyalist and willing partner in the crime against Falun Gong, to become Hu's successor. However, Jiang was still able to get Zhou Yongkang, another of his henchman with blood on his hands, to replace Luo Gan at the top position in the Politburo Standing Committee and guarantee that the persecution of Falun Gong would be continued. Jiang's next step was to initiate a scheme with Zhou and Bo to plan a coup to get rid of Xi Jinping in 2014.

(4) The boiling over of grievances from the people

Today, China is brimming with discontent and turmoil. It is not only the direct consequence of the CCP's persecution of Falun Gong, but also an unfortunate situation deliberately manufactured by the Politics and Law Committee.

According to China's official statistics, before the CCP's crackdown on Falun Gong, there were one hundred million people practicing Falun Gong. In the beginning of the persecution, the CCP utilized all its propaganda tools to broadcast 24-hour continual programs to demonize Falun Gong. However, none of the planned programs so much as alluded to Falun Gong practitioners as having committed corruption, prostitution, petty theft, murder, or arson. This omission in the broadcasts precisely gave proof that Falun Gong practitioners who live their lives in accordance with the tenets of "truthfulness, compassion, and forbearance," are all good citizens.

It can be said that to suppress such a large group of the population, Jiang's evil intention cannot be achieved as long as there is a hint of social justice. In a normal society, freedom of speech, freedom of belief, freedom of the press, freedom of assembly, freedom to protest and demonstrate, freedom to have an independent judiciary and so on, are means of maintaining social justice. The primary task of the "610 Office" is to be an obstacle that hinders social justice and stunt its development.

In this way, the Chinese society is turned into a jungle where "the survival of the fittest" and "the strong will devour the weak" rule, where there is no opportunity for victims to voice or redress their grievances. These grievances grow ever bigger and accumulate, creating a situation similar to a pressure cooker that can explode at any time.

It is precisely such a scenario that the Politics and Law Committee needs, since the more chaotic the society, the more attention and responsibility the people will entrust to the Politics and Law Committee, and the more resources the committee is able to obtain. When the entire Communist regime has to rely on persecuting Falun Gong practitioners to maintain its existence, the Politics and Law Committee will naturally become the highest controlling authority. Currently, it costs the country a staggering 700 billion yuan RMB [~112 billion USD] annually to maintain the CCP's stability. This sum is more than the allocated government military expenditure. [9] As the Politics and Law Committee may be required to mobilize the armed police at any time to suppress civil commotions, and military mobilization procedures are complex, this makes the expansion of power for the Politics and Law Committee possible in order to contend with the Military Commission.

Jiang Zemin exploited the Politics and Law Committee as the vehicle to promote Bo Xilai's rise in power, this is precisely because it supplied the only possible guarantee for Bo to hold absolute power.

Conclusion

From instituting the "610 Office" in 1999, to coercing the re-election of Jiang Zemin as Chairman of the Military Committee in 2002; from deliberately adding two more members to the Politburo Standing Committee, to be in charge of "politics and law" and "publicity and propaganda," respectively, during the 2002 16th National Congress, to abolishing Hu Jintao's core power by changing the Standing Committee into an "oligarchy" mode of operation; from strengthening the Politburo Standing Committee's powers and increased "stability maintenance" expenditure by the creation of a second central authority, to the detailed planning of assassinations and coups; the CCP's reorganizations of the power structure in the last 15 years have all been designed to safeguard the resources it can access for the persecution.

The CCP monopolizes all public resources and possesses absolute power without restrictions, while the international community continues to invest large amounts of capital into China through investment, trade, and good relations. Be that as it may, the expenditures for this persecution and the related issues that are generated are such that even China, the world's second highest GDP economy, is overwhelmed.

Since the premise of the persecution of Falun Gong is to allow the mechanism that upholds society to fail completely by encouraging evil actions and attacking the compassionate and kind, therefore the victims are not just Falun Gong practitioners, but also ordinary people who are all faced with the loss of social security. Currently, government officials and the general public are in opposing camps. Then, there is also the issue of environmental and social problems brought about by a nationwide moral decay—all of which are directly related to the persecution.

In ancient Chinese history, four different emperors had taken calamitous measures to annihilate Buddhism, but none of these incidents lasted over six years or covered more than a limited geographic area. In the West, likewise, was the intermittent persecution of Christians by the Roman Empire. However, regardless of whether it is ancient China or the Roman Empire, neither had the capability to control every aspect of society, nor the indemnity of a full range of organizational and financial security, unlike the CCP. Additionally, the CCP has the power to pour the entire nation's resources to focus exclusively on the persecution, with an array of extreme torture methods and brainwashing, as well as the guaranteed protection of the army and armed police when undertaking large-scale and systematic organ harvesting of Falun Gong practitioners—resulting in murder for profit.

Seventeen years of persecution and counter-persecution activities, the situation has been evidently clear; Falun Gong's protests against the persecution will continue and persist, while the CCP's regime is not able to sustain its status quo and is on the verge of disintegration.

In human history, there has never been an empire that spanned over a thousand years, but there have been faiths that lasted for more than a millennium. No matter how utterly devoid of conscience the persecution seems, good and evil retribution will eventually become apparent.

[1] Kyodo News correspondent reports from Beijing, states: "It seems in addition to being investigated for corruption, Zhou Yongkang will likely have to face inquiries about the coup."

http://www.bbc.co.uk/zhongwen/simp/china/2014/07/140730_zhou_yongkang_japan.shtml

[2] CNNIC announced the international export distribution of China's Internet Network (CIN) at the end of June 2013. The total international export bandwidth of CIN's principal internet backbone network reached 2,098,150 Mbps.

http://data.lmtw.com/yjjg/201307/91967.html

[3] Harvard University's proxy testing shows that Falun Gong-related websites met with the most severe blockade by the CCP

http://cyber.law.harvard.edu/publications/2005/Internet_Filtering_in_China_in_2004_2005

https://opennet.net/studies/china#toc4a

[4] A collection of the World Organization to Investigate the Persecution of Falun Gong investigation reports

http://www.zhuichaguoji.org/node/23256

[5] Investigative report on the "610 Office" systematic involvement in the persecution of Falun Gong

http://www.zhuichaguoji.org/node/23202

[6] Inside the Ring

http://www.washingtontimes.com/news/2001/mar/09/20010309-021538-9115r/

[7] In 2002, Liu Jing disclosed internal divergence in the CCP leadership regarding the repression of Falun Gong

http://www.epochtimes.com/gb/12/4/9/n3560912.htm

[8] The secret behind Hu Jintao's three hair-raising assassination encounters

http://www.epochtimes.com/gb/12/5/27/n3598251.htm

[9] The National People's Congress and the Chinese People's Political Consultative Conference views on Chinese military spending and the "stability maintenance" expenses

http://www.bbc.co.uk/zhongwen/simp/china/2014/03/140305_ana_china_npc_army.shtml

Persecuting the Peaceful:
A Political Response

By Edward McMillan-Scott

In 2006, Beijing was preparing to host the 2008 Olympics, and I was visiting the city in my capacity as the European Parliament's Vice-President for Human Rights & Democracy. China was preparing to show the world that it was a responsible world power that had progressed economically and politically. Liu Jingmin, Vice-President of the Beijing Olympic Bid Committee, had said that allowing Beijing to host the Games would "help the development of human rights". In a dingy hotel room with the curtains drawn, I learnt the truth behind China's facade of progress.

In reality, China had hardened its crackdown on political and religious dissent in advance of the games. Practitioners of Falun Gong—a peaceful spiritual practice that combines meditation with the cultivation of the key virtues of truthfulness, compassion and forbearance—had been brutally repressed since 1999, when the Chinese Communist Party (CCP) became fearful the movement would become an organized force that could threaten the Party. I learnt that the Chinese regime had descended into genocide.

Those I met in 2006—some former prisoners of conscience, reformers and dissidents, told me of the brutal persecution they and their families had faced at the hands of the CCP. I spoke with Niu Jinping, who had served two years in prison for practicing Falun Gong. His wife Zhang Lianying was still in prison and he was in charge of caring for their two-year-old daughter. The last time he had seen his wife, her entire body was bruised from the repeated beatings she took as the torturers tried to make her denounce Falun Gong. Following her release from prison she sent me a list of '50 torture' steps that the prison guards used to try and make her renounce Falun Gong. The beating she endured was so severe she fell into a coma while in prison.

Most horrifically, the men confirmed what I had only heard whispered until then—the Chinese regime was forcefully harvesting the organs of imprisoned Falun Gong practitioners, for sale to the booming organ transplant industry. Cao Dong, who had also been imprisoned for practicing Falun Gong, told me tearfully, that he saw the cadaver of his friend—a fellow practitioner—in the prison hospital with holes where the organs had been removed.

The following month, former Canadian MP David Kilgour and human rights lawyer David Matas published a report examining the allegations of forced organ harvesting from Falun Gong practitioners who had been imprisoned—the first of its kind. The report concluded bleakly that "there has been, and continues today to be, large-scale organ seizures from unwilling Falun Gong practitioners." A year later, Manfred Nowak, the United Nations Special Rapporteur on Torture issued a report that corroborated Kilgour and Matas' findings. It stated that: "Organ harvesting has been inflicted on a large number of unwilling Falun Gong practitioners at a wide variety of locations for the purpose of making available organs for transplant operations."

Following my meetings in Beijing, all those I met were detained by the CCP. Some went missing, some were tortured. At that time, no statements were made by national European leaders, fearful of offending the rising economic superpower.

Since then, the world's attitude to China has shifted. In the run-up to the 2008 Olympics, I led an international boycott of the Games in view of China's repeated human rights abuses. Several high profile figures joined the boycott. US film director Steven Spielberg and the UK's Prince Charles refused to attend the ceremony, as did the President of the European Parliament, the President of the European Commission and the EU's Foreign Affairs Commissioner. Internationally renowned artist Ai Weiwei—who co-designed the Bird's Nest stadium where the Olympic Games took place—voiced his support for the boycott, calling the regime of his home country 'disgusting'.

I have continued to campaign for reform in China. In the European Parliament, members have adopted several resolutions calling on China to respect human rights and end the brutal persecution of the Falun Gong. I have hosted several high profile events to maintain focus on this issue. In January 2013, I welcomed into the Parliament, Enver Tohti, an ex-surgeon from China who gave a powerful testimony describing how he had been forced to remove the organs of an executed prisoner while he was still alive.

The Parliament maintains constant pressure on the EU's foreign policy chief, Catherine Ashton, to raise human rights issues and trade dialogues with China. Indeed, the promotion of trade and human rights need not be mutually exclusive; Germany has seen an explosive growth in trade with China over the last decade, but has also taken a robust approach to human rights.

The US has also become much more critical of China and its disregard for human rights. In the run-up to the 24th anniversary of the Tiananmen Square massacre, where thousands of protesters were brutally suppressed by the CCP, the US State Department issued a statement calling on the Chinese government to end harassment of participants and vindicate the victims. The US Congress is also taking a firmer stand. In advance of Obama's June visit to China, Chairman of the Foreign Affairs Committee, Robert Menendez wrote an open letter to President Obama, urging him to raise the issue of China's continued human rights abuses, including the Government's persecution of the Falun Gong.

Tough words have often been matched with tough action. In early 2011, blind Chinese dissident Chen Guangcheng escaped the CCP's house arrest and travelled to the US embassy in Beijing. Much to China's displeasure, he was given refuge in the US embassy and received support in his battle against the Chinese Government. A spokesperson from China's Ministry of Foreign Affairs railed against US involvement in the Chen case, demanding an apology and warning the US from interfering in China's domestic matters in such a way again. Chen Guangcheng now lives as a free man in the US with his wife and daughter, and the emptiness of China's threats has been made apparent.

To maintain the momentum on human rights in China, Chen Guangcheng and I have launched a transatlantic alliance on human rights and democracy in Washington and Brussels. The Defending Freedoms Project, in association with Amnesty International and ChinaAid, calls on members of the European Parliament and US congressmen and women to adopt and advocate on behalf of prisoners of conscience from around the world—several high profile Chinese prisoners of conscience are on the list. Gao Zhisheng, the Christian human rights lawyer who took up the cause of Falun Gong in 2005—and who stayed for many years in prison—is my choice.

At the Washington launch of the initiative, I had the privilege of seeing again my old friend Niu Jinping, whom I had not seen since our initial meeting in the Beijing hotel room in 2006. Like

Chen, he is now enjoying life as a free man with his family in the US, but also continuing his fight for a free and just China. His wife Zhang Lianying had apparently made a full recovery since the horrors she experienced at the hands of the CCP.

Throughout history, there has not been a single authoritarian regime, which has not crumbled in the end. International political support has highlighted the cracks in China's system of brutal repression. Continued and enhanced support for those harassed, imprisoned and tortured by the regime will help them in their struggle for the basic rights and freedoms many take for granted. We must not waver now.

Brainwashing: Extermination of Mind and Body

By Xia Yiyang

From the onset, the persecution of Falun Gong by the Chinese Communist Party (CCP) has not acted as an implementation of law, but rather a political campaign to persecute spiritual beliefs. At the core of this political campaign is the goal of "transforming" deep spiritual beliefs through intense psychological torture or brainwashing.

The order to transform through brainwashing came from the very top

Within 20 days of the start of the persecution on July 20, 1999, the CCP Central Committee issued two documents targeting Falun Gong practitioners who were also CCP members for brainwashing[1]. On August 24, 1999, a third document, jointly issued by the General Office of the CCP Central and the General Office of the State Council, expanded the use of brainwashing on all Falun Gong practitioners. It elevated the importance of such brainwashing to be the "important measure for the effectiveness and the victory of this struggle (against Falun Gong)."

All three documents stipulated that, "if one does not come to the 'correct understanding,' i.e. giving up one's belief in 'truthfulness, compassion, tolerance,' the basic principles of Falun Gong, one cannot be "released" even if this person was only seeking fitness [through the practice]."

The head of the "CCP Central Committee Leading Group for Handling the Falun Gong issues" has and continues to be directly in charge of carrying out brainwashing.

Luo Gan, then deputy head and later head of the leading group, gave speeches focused on brainwashing and strongly promoted the so-called "Masanjia [labor camp] experience[2]." In September 2000, the CCP Central 610 Office—a secret agency created for the sole purpose of persecuting Falun Gong practitioners—established the "education and transformation work (directing and coordinating) team" to focus on the nationwide brainwashing activities. The team was headed by Li Dongsheng, then deputy director of the CCP Central 610 Office. In September 2009, Li became the director of the CCP Central 610 Office and remained in that position until December 2013, when Li was purged and investigated for a serious legal violation.

Transformation standards

Transformation through brainwashing does not simply mean giving up the practice. The earliest transformation standards appeared in the Notice by the "Two Offices" on August 24, 1999[3]. Then, Masanjia Forced Labor Camp came up with a set of standards. The head of the CCP Central 610 Office, Wang Maolin, introduced these standards at the "Ministry of Justice Education and Transformation Work Sharing and Award Meeting" held on August 29, 2000. There are five standards to which Falun Gong practitioners must adhere: relinquish the practice, write the repentance statement, submit all Falun Gong books and materials, write testimonials against Falun Gong and the founder and transform other practitioners.

If any one standard is not met, one is not considered to be transformed. Transformation is the way that leads to leniency, shortening one's term, serving one's term outside the prison or labor camp and being released before serving the full term[4]. That is to say, reeducation through labor had nothing to do with "illegal actions," but targeted entirely one's spiritual beliefs. In September 2000, the CCP Central 610 Office officially promulgated the Masanjia transformation standards to the entire country[5].

Failures in ideology inevitably lead to violence

The CCP's punishing system is different from that of democratic countries because of the element of "thought reform." However, the brainwashing of Falun Gong practitioners differs from the thought reforms of the political persecutions throughout the history of the CCP's rule, both in the methods used by the perpetrators and the impact of such methods on their victims.

The CCP's ideology was constructed as a hybrid of Marxism-Leninism combined with Mao's theories. In the early years of its rule, carried by the residual of the "victorious" Revolution, the CCP's ideology still had the power of misleading and intimidating at the same time. Most of the people being reformed did not have a sophisticated belief system of their own and thus passively accepted the new doctrine; many others had illusions of the CCP, thus tried to persuade themselves to be reformed, even though it was not out of their free will.

Falun Gong, however, is totally different. Rooted in traditional Chinese culture, Falun Gong provides a completely different set of values and world view; The practitioners benefit from this cultivation mentally and physically, thus won't be influenced and confused by CCP's propaganda.

On the other hand, while the practice of communism has already failed around the world, the CCP has lost much of its early ideology, turning instead to an interest driven entity. With little ability to capture the hearts of the Chinese people, the CCP turned to violent reform, such as brainwashing, to keep its rule. Party officials believed they could crush the Falun Gong movement within days, but practitioners' moral fortitude and courage has proved too powerful.

The locations and perpetrators of brainwashing

Transformation quotas are given to prisons, labor camps, brainwashing centers, work units and neighborhoods. Specific personnel is assigned to carry out the transformation work. The labor camps were the CCP's first choice as the locations for transformation.

On October 29, 1999, Masanjia Forced Labor Camp (Formally Masanjia Re-education through Labor Camp) located in Shenyang, Liaoning province, setup the "Female No. 2 Brigade" to house Falun Gong practitioners[6]. It is the most notorious site in the persecution of Falun Gong.

Since the start, Masanjia Labor Camp was selected by the CCP Central 610 Office to carry out brainwashing trials. The abusive techniques and manipulations practiced at Masanjia were then promoted across China. According to the former director of the Shenyang Municipal Bureau of Justice, Han Guangsheng, Masanjia has only one brainwashing tool—the electric baton[7]. In actuality, Masanjia has implemented a few dozen torture methods on Falun Gong practitioners.

Beijing is a good example. According to media reports, the city was "faced with tremendous difficulties and setbacks in its work to transform Falun Gong practitioners." Eventually, it was the Beijing Bureau of Reeducation through Labor that "found a way to overcome the difficulties."

The Beijing Bureau of Reeducation through Labor was awarded the highest honor by the Ministry of Justice for its brainwashing techniques. It became the "advanced unit in anti-Falun Gong work" in Beijing. Most guards in China's forced labor system are not trained to do ideological work. How could the least qualified guards solve the problem that all Party officials and the ideological professionals failed?

Wang Maolin, the head of the CCP Central 610 Office offered a realistic explanation of Beijing's success: strict management, an isolated environment and the "forceful nature of the reeducation through labor system[8]." Those who are familiar with the situation in China's labor camps and CCP's terminology understand that the latter refers to violence and torture.

Since the isolation and ongoing violence and torture in the labor camps could not be applied directly to the society, in 2000, the CCP Central 610 Office started to promote "study sessions" in similarly secluded venues. In 2001, these sessions were given the new title of "Legal Education Centers," i.e., brainwashing centers, and were highly promoted across the country[9].

These Legal Education Centers are like prisons and labor camps, but are set up by local non-law enforcement authorities. It is worth noting that in over ten years, over 400 such brainwashing centers were established throughout the country. While they do not belong to any government or law enforcement agencies, they are neither part of any civil organizations. They have no legality and are not registered anywhere. No documents were issued by either the Party or the State to define their affiliation and mission. As a result, without being subject to any legal oversight or regulation, staff at these extrajudicial education centers freely arrests, detains, tortures and even kills at will.

In addition to the aforementioned major brainwashing facilities, i.e. labor camps and brainwashing centers, CCP officials at all levels actively carry out brainwashing within the society at large. The Chaoyang district in Beijing once had 720 so-called "education assistant" teams. Furthermore, under the planning of CCP Central, corporate enterprises, the Women's Union, the Communist Youth League, scientific communities, scholars, and educators have all participated in the brainwashing of Falun Gong practitioners one way or another.

Evidence of brainwashing noted throughout the persecution

The earliest record of brainwashing occurred before the nationwide persecution began in July 1999. After the April 25, 1999 peaceful appeal in Beijing by Falun Gong practitioners, the CCP's highest ranking officials franticly prepared for the crackdown. The former director of PLA 301 Hospital, Li Qihua, wrote a letter about how he had benefited mentally and physically from practicing Falun Gong and how beneficial it could be to the country and the people of China. The letter was titled "The shallow understanding of Falun Gong by a veteran member of Red Army and CCP." Upon reading this letter, then vice chairman of the CCP Central Military Commission (CMC) Zhang Wannian, immediately reported to Jiang Zemin. Jiang then wrote a long letter to the Politburo, Secretariat and CMC leadership[10].

In the following few days, Zhang began to send officers to speak with Li Qihua on a daily basis. They attempted to make Li give up his belief in Falun Gong by exhausting him with non-stop conversations. In the end, they even fabricated a "regret" paper[11]. The letter Jiang sent earlier became an official document issued by the Office of the CCP Central Committee (No.[1999]19) on May 23. The document detailed the transformation of Falun Gong practitioners who were also CCP members[12].

The CCP Central 610 Office issued the "Points to implement the education and transformation battle" in September 2000,[13] to carry out the transformation to all Falun Gong practitioners across the country.

Since then, brainwashing has become the most important daily task for all levels of the CCP Committees. Hebei province, one of the focused regions for brainwashing, spent 15 million yuan in 2001 to establish brainwashing centers in 11 municipalities and various counties[14].

April 25, 2001, the CCP Central Organization Department issued a document detailing the experiences in the struggle against Falun Gong by Masanjia Labor Camp, the Beijing Bureau of Reeducation through Labor, and Qitaihe CCP Committee (Heilongjiang province). The document focused on transformation[15].

In addition, the CCP Central 610 Office also organized special campaigns. In 2010, it started a "2010-2012 Transformation-Through-Reeducation Assault and Consolidation Overall Battle Work Plan," which triggered a new round of brainwashing of Falun Gong practitioners nationwide[16].

When the three-year battle ended, the Central 610 Office immediately started another one for the next three years. From the goals set for this current round, one can see that the CCP's struggle against Falun Gong had already failed. For instance, one region set a goal such that "by the end of 2015, those already 'transformed' will remain transformed." Another goal was to ensure that "during the final battle period there should be no new Falun Gong members."

The immorality of brainwashing

For Party and State officials at various levels, transformation of Falun Gong practitioners is mandatory and directly connected to their performance. To meet their goals, the most commonly used method is organizing many people to target a single victim. This method was suggested in the Notice by the "Two Offices" back in August 1999. The Notice says: "one should use the '1 on 1, more on 1' method."

The Chuncheng neighborhood office of Lvyuan district, in the city of Changchun in Liaoning province implemented a "6-on-1" method by mobilizing an official from the neighborhood, a regular official, the secretary of the neighborhood office, a police officer, a family member, and a co-worker to force one Falun Gong practitioner to transform. An enterprise affiliated with the Tonghua Steel and Iron Group in Jilin province set the record of "20-on-1."[17]

The number of Falun Gong practitioners in a region is used as the base number when calculating the transformation rate. Those in labor camps are not included in the base number. Therefore, in order to reach the target transformation rate, some regions send practitioners who refuse to give up the practice to labor camps or sentence them to prisons.

January 17, 2001, Falun Gong practitioner Liu Yan from Qingan County, Heilongjiang province was caught and severely beaten before being sent to Huaihua Forced Labor Camp for a year and a half. At first, the labor camp refused to accept the badly wounded Liu. The police had to "twist somebody's arm" to persuade the labor camp. On July 21, 2002, Liu Yan was persecuted to death.

In order to reach the transformation rate, the CCP Laiwu Committee secretary in Shandong province, Li Yumei, would bribe and coerce labor camps to accept Falun Gong practitioners who refused to give up the practice and would otherwise not be accepted by the camps due to the physical conditions. It is fairly common for officials to bribe the labor camp to accept Falun Gong practitioners to meet the transformation rate.

Because the brainwashing centers, labor camps and prisons all must meet the transformation rate, they all resort to torture methods to meet their quotas.

There were indeed tyrannies, collective punishments, sometimes even punishment by family extermination in Chinese history, but no one would make family members kill each other, or force someone to betray one's teacher for self-interest. Chinese traditional culture teaches respect for one's teacher, thus the saying "Teacher for one day, Father for an entire life." Students under the same teacher are considered belonging to the same family.

Yet the transformation tactics used against Falun Gong practitioners are forcing one to not only sell out one's teacher and fellow students, but also self-incriminate. Essentially, transformation is the extermination of one's conscience and soul. Those who refuse to be transformed are constantly subject to various methods of torture. To force a human being, through torture no less, to give up a cultivation practice that improves one's spiritual and moral nature is the real crime and an act of shame for any civilized society.

Violence and brainwashing emerged during the early years of the persecution. A high-ranking CCP official revealed to the Washington Post that the early stage of persecution was not at all successful, until an "effective approach" was found in 2001. This effective approach includes three aspects: violence, high-pressure propaganda and brainwashing classes. The anti-Falun Gong campaign worked only when all three aspects were used, with the greatest emphasis placed on brainwashing classes.

Yet it was not only the brainwashing of Falun Gong practitioners that was utilized in an attempt to extinguish the group. The public also needed to be deceived and coerced into believing that Falun Gong was dangerous so as to elicit support for the CCP's illegal actions. The first major propaganda stunt was a staged self-immolation of falsely-identified Falun Gong practitioners on Tiananmen Square, January 23, 2001. Violence and brainwashing became a policy to be systematically implemented.

In the climate of intense propaganda, the image of 12-year-old Liu Siying's "burnt" body and the video of people falsely identified as Falun Gong practitioners saying that they would ascend to heaven after self-immolation, were continuously broadcast for days on end. It was after the staged event that violence and brainwashing became a policy to be systematically implemented. When people were misled into believing CCP's lies, the legitimacy of violent brainwashing was then secured[18].

Falun Gong practitioner Zhang Yijie worked at the Ministry of Foreign Trade and Economic Cooperation, now called the Ministry of Commerce. Zhang was sent to Beijing Female Labor Camp and was held in solitary confinement for an extended period of time because she refused to give up her practice. On a number of occasions, she was locked up in a small dark room for several consecutive days. The first time she was placed in seclusion, Zhang was deprived of sleep for 18 days and nights. The second time, in order to make her sign a "Repentance Statement" (document that proves practitioners have given up their practice by expressing remorse for practicing Falun Gong, renouncing the practice and guaranteeing that they will never associate with other practitioners or go to Beijing to appeal on behalf of the practice), the guards forced her to remain standing for 42 days and nights. In addition, Zhang was subject to food and water restriction, sleep deprivation, limited use of the restroom and other forms of torture. In the end, Zhang was almost blind, could hardly speak and her hair turned white. But she never gave up her belief in Falun Gong.

The CCP's official media reports confirm the widespread use of torture to brainwash practitioners. A website under the Beijing Bureau of Justice reported on how a Falun Gong practitioner was transformed in Beijing Female Labor Camp: "[a]fter 16 days and nights of non-stop work, Du finally wrote the statement to give up the [Falun Gong] practice...."

The inhumane nature of the transformation methods used against Falun Gong practitioners is well-illustrated in the forced participation by practitioners' family members. At the February 27, 2001 Press Conference of the State Council Information Office, Liu Jing, then director of the CCP Central 610 Office offered a chilling example of a woman in Shandong province who "voluntarily" sent her husband to the notorious Masanjia Forced Labor Camp, and reportedly pleaded with the guards to "help" her own husband!

Lin Chengtao was an assistant researcher at Peking Union Medical College of the Chinese Medical University Basic Medical Sciences Institute. Lin was one of the main researchers of the "863 Plan" and China Medical Board project. In October 2001, Lin was sent to Beijing Tuanhe Labor Camp for refusing to give up Falun Gong. Lin was put through many types of torture, including corporal punishment, repeated psychological brainwashing, solitary confinement and electrocution with three 30,000 volt electric batons administered simultaneously. All these did not make him give up his belief in Falun Gong. Towards the end of 2001, Lin's wife, who was transformed by Beijing Xin'an (Female) Labor Camp, wrote a letter to Tuanhe Labor Camp suggesting that they use electric batons, beatings, mental agitation, and sleep deprivation to force her husband to transform. Lin was forced to repetitively read his wife's letter until, in the end, he could not withstand such mental torture and "went insane"[20].

Strictly speaking, every Falun Gong practitioner who was persecuted to death died because they refused to give up their beliefs. Based on the list of deaths published by minghui.org, the incomplete statistics of 588 deaths, until April 30, 2004 in Heilongjiang, Jilin, Liaoning, Shandong and Hebei province, shows that 232 persons (40%) had "refused to be transformed" as the direct cause of death. Among them, 213 (91.8%) were tortured to death.

The CCP requires a 100 percent transformation rate of all Falun Gong practitioners. Such a policy forces practitioners to choose between giving up their belief or suffering horrendous acts of torture. To a firm believer, the former signifies spiritual death while the latter is likely to lead to physical death. Brainwashing is therefore the deliberate extermination of Falun Gong.

Brainwashing propels the collapse of morality

The first person to carry out brainwashing in the labor camp system was Zhou Kaidong, former head of the Beijing Bureau of Reeducation through Labor. Zhou later was sentenced to 15 years in prison for taking bribes.

This is not an isolated case, but instead a very common phenomenon. The recent shake-ups among high level CCP officials implicate everyone who has played a key role in ordering and intensifying the persecution. Corruption permeates all layers within the regime, from Jiang Zemin, to Zhou Yongkang, former head of the Political and Legal Affairs Committee to Li Dongsheng, former head of the CCP Central 610 Office. No wonder, in the words of Wang Lijun, former director of public security and vice mayor of Chongqing, they want to "hunt down and kill all" Falun Gong practitioners who follow the principles of "truth, compassion and tolerance."

The CCP attempts to use morally depraved individuals to transform Falun Gong practitioners—who only aspire to be good, benevolent people—into corrupted, empty shells, just like the CCP itself. Every year, the CCP rewards those who actively intensify the persecution. By honoring those who use violent manipulation against good people, the CCP has forced Chinese people to live within a completely inverted value system of right and wrong.

---

[1] Li Lanqing's letter to the "Ministry of Justice Reeducation and Transformation Experience Sharing and Commendation Conference" (August 29, 2000)

[2] Luo Gan's speech at the "Ministry of Justice Reeducation and Transformation Experience Sharing and Commendation Conference" (August 29, 2000)

[3] The People's Daily, August 25, 1999, page 4. Notice from the Office of the CCP Central Committee and the Office of the State Council on Improving Education and Transformation of Falun Gong; http://www.peopledaily.com.cn/rmrb/199908/25/newfiles/wzb_19990825001026_4.html

[4] Wang Maolin's speech at the "Ministry of Justice Reeducation and Transformation Experience Sharing and Commendation Conference" (August 29, 2000)

[5] Opinions of the Office of the Central Leadership team on Handling Falun Gong Issues on Instigating Reeducation Transformation Crackdown Campaign (September 22, 2000)

[6] sina.com, June 15, 2001, "On the director of Masanjia Labor Camp Female No.2 Brigade, Su Jing"

[7] minghui.org, July 4, 2005, Former Director of Shenyang Bureau of Justice exposing secrets of 610 Office; http://www.minghui.org/mh/articles/2005/7/4/105408.html

[8] Wang Maolin's speech at the "Ministry of Justice Reeducation and Transformation Experience Sharing and Commendation Conference" (August 29, 2000)

[9] Opinions of the Office of the Central Leadership team on Handling Falun Gong Issues on Instigating Reeducation Transformation Crackdown Campaign (September 22, 2000)

Opinions of the Office of the Central Leadership team on Handling Falun Gong Issues on Intensifying the education and transformation work. (April 9, 2001)

[10] Biography of Zhang Wannian

[11] minghui.org, Truth behind People's Daily Li Qihua's self-criminating statement

http://package.minghui.org/zhenxiang_ziliao/ziliao_huibian/fake_report/2_24.html

[12] CCP Hebei Provincial Office Notice [1999 No.21] to Follow the Notice from CCP Central Office [1999 No.19]

[13] Opinions of the Office of the Central Leadership team on Handling Falun Gong Issues on Instigating Reeducation Transformation Crackdown Campaign (September 22, 2000)

[14] CCP Hebei provincial office document [2002 No.5]

[15] CCP Central Organization Department Document on the experiences in the struggle against Falun Gong by Masanjia Labor Camp, Beijing Bureau of Reeducation through Labor, and Qitaihe city CCP Committee, April 25, 2001

[16] CECC 2011 Annual Report.

http://www.cecc.gov/publications/annual-reports/2011-annual-report

[17] All reference in this section come from the report at www.zhuichaguoji.org/node/123

[18] Torture Is Breaking Falun Gong; China Systematically Eradicating Group: John Pomfret and Philip P. Pan. The Washington Post. Washington, D.C.: Aug 5, 2001. pg. A.01

[19] minghui.org, Record of persecution of Zhang Yijie by the CCP; http://www.minghui.org/mh/articles/2008/9/3/185228.html

[20] minghui.org, Jan. 1, 2003, "Relentless Brainwashing created tragedy: young scholar driven insane, wife brainwashed wanting to torture husband"; http://www.minghui.org/mh/articles/2003/1/1/42004.html

Brutality Unmasked: The Shocking Truth About Forced Organ Harvesting in China

By Katrina Lantos Swett, J.D., Ph.D.

In our sophisticated age, the word "evil" has become somewhat unfashionable. Because it leaves no room for excuses, justification or compromise, it is a word that understandably makes people uncomfortable. And yet, there are some atrocities that can be described in no other way. The Chinese Communist Party's (CCP) practice of involuntary organ harvesting from prisoners of conscience is truly evil and it is time for physicians, political leaders and human rights activists to join together to tell the truth about this barbaric crime.

Although the CCP has gone to extraordinary lengths to try and conceal the reality of this brutal practice, the truth is slowly beginning to emerge. It is a nightmarish portrait in which human beings are treated as commodities that can be eliminated at will and their very organs exploited for the financial advantage of others.

What began in the 1980's with the clearly unethical harvesting of organs from executed criminals, eventually devolved into a far more sinister undertaking. It is difficult to pinpoint precisely when the moral line was breached between stealing organs from dead murderers and rapists, to actually murdering political prisoners and prisoners of conscience in order to harvest and sell their organs. But the evidence is compelling that this line has in fact been crossed on a massive scale.

Thanks to the remarkable work of the NGO, Doctors Against Forced Organ Harvesting (DAFOH), the sordid and heartbreaking tale of greed and political repression, is beginning to emerge. Based on extensive documentation from interviews with former prisoners, staff from labor camps and even medical personnel who have been complicit in these human rights abuses, it appears that tens of thousands of innocent people may have been victims of this crime against humanity.

And who are these innocent victims? The evidence suggests that a high proportion of them are Falun Gong practitioners. This peaceful community of believers has been the target of a brutal government campaign of repression, vilification, imprisonment and torture, dating back to 1999. Like other religious communities including Tibetan Buddhists and the House church movement, the Falun Gong is perceived as an unacceptable threat to the social dominance of the CCP. Because faith based communities are bound together by shared beliefs in laws and principles that transcend the temporal and the material, they are viewed with deep suspicion and fear by regimes such as the Communist government in China. No single religious community in China has suffered from this suspicion more than the Falun Gong. For more than 15 years, this community has responded to this brutal persecution through peaceful and non-violent resistance, coupled with a heroic and determined commitment to their beliefs and practices.

It has always been baffling to the rest of the world that the Chinese government would target this traditional, spiritual practice of the Buddha school. With their gentle, meditative exercises and a moral philosophy that emphasizes compassion, truth and tolerance, the Falun Gong are truly model citizens in every community in which they live. At one time this faith community was actually welcomed by Chinese authorities for their admirable morality and ethics. But as the Falun Gong grew in popularity, with as many as 70-100 million practitioners, the Chinese authorities grew fearful that this spiritual movement represented a threat to the Communist party's monopoly over the hearts and minds of the Chinese people.

The Chinese government has also used the vast resources of their propaganda machinery to target Falun Gong practitioners for widespread persecution. Despite the enormous suffering they have endured, the Falun Gong have remained steadfast in their beliefs and committed to telling their stories. While dozens of China's leading human rights lawyers and activists have been motivated to speak out on behalf of the Falun Gong, the practitioners themselves have channeled the power of the internet to create tools that have outsmarted the Chinese internet police and shared their stories with the world. The Falun Gong have played a central role in helping the Chinese people break through the Great Firewall of China that keeps its nearly billion citizens from freely accessing the internet. Some of the most sophisticated and effective firewall circumvention tools, such as Freegate and Ultrasurf, have been created by Falun Gong practitioners who believe that unfettered access to uncensored information is essential to building a democratic and decent future for the people of China.

Thanks in part to internet freedom tools such as these, information about the nightmare of criminal organ harvesting is getting out of China as well as into China, creating a growing movement to expose and eliminate this massive abuse of basic human rights.

In December of 2013, DAFOH delivered a petition with 1.5

million signatures to the UN High Commissioner for Human Rights, urging that an investigation be conducted into China's "slaughter of prisoners of conscience for organ procurement".

Thereafter, the European Parliament passed a resolution demanding an immediate end to China's state sanctioned organ harvesting from executed prisoners of conscience, including Falun Gong.

These are important and encouraging steps, but realistically, a challenging road lies ahead to successfully stamp out illegal organ procurement. Part of the reason for this is pure greed. In a world where there is a shortage of freely donated organs available for transplant, desperate patients are willing to pay massive sums of money to obtain a needed organ. Kidneys can sell for $60,000 and livers have been reported to command sums of nearly $100,000. Corneas, hearts and lungs are also in great demand. It is the toxic combination of political targeting, financial greed and profound corruption that has created this medical and moral nightmare. By some estimates, as many as 65,000 Falun Gong may have been victims of this perfect storm of evil.

Now, as China faces a period of political transition, there is evidence that those who have been involved in massive human rights abuses against the Falun Gong are determined to be succeeded by politicians who themselves are implicated in these crimes. Why? Because they want to ensure that they will have impunity for the wrongs they have done. These individuals would do well to remember the words of Martin Luther King, "The arc of history is long but it bends towards justice".

Adlai Stevenson II, former Ambassador to the United Nations and Governor of Illinois, once said that "solutions begin by telling the truth". It is time for leaders around the world to insist on truth telling when it comes to the matter of involuntary organ harvesting. The Chinese government must not be permitted to sweep this crime under the rug and above all this practice must be stopped, once and for all. It has been observed that "In any compromise between good and evil, it is only evil that can profit". There has already been far too much profiting on the part of evil as a result of the abhorrent harvesting of organs from innocent men and women across China. Their stolen lives cry out for justice and it is a cry that must not go unheeded.

Silent Atrocities

By Teng Biao

"*Four electric batons began to shock me and I felt them as they hit their mark. It was as though my internal organs and all the muscles were jumping around underneath my skin, trying to escape or hide. I was rolling on the floor in agony. When Wang began to shock my penis, I begged him for mercy. My cries for mercy instead prompted laughter and even more flagrant torture.*

"*Didn't you say the CCP used torture? This time we'll give you the full experience again. Torturing Falun Gong—that's true, totally true. These twelve sets that we're using on you, we learned from [torturing] Falun Gong. I'm not afraid of you speaking the truth—in fact I defy you to write it. The chances of you surviving to tell the tale are next to nothing. After we kill you, they'll never find your body.*"

I lost track of time when someone began to urinate on my face. Three sets of electric batons shocked me as I rolled on the floor, bereft of dignity. After ten or so minutes, my entire body was shaking, unable to stop. Afterwards, I was shackled, kneeling on the ground as they used a toothpick to poke at my genitals. I cannot use language to express the hopelessness, pain and despair. In there, human language and emotion have not even the slightest power.*"

Gao Zhisheng, lawyer

One: Silence in the face of horrendous violence

The above is an excerpt of Gao Zhisheng's description of the torture he suffered, written in his recent essay, *"Dark Night, Dark Hood and Kidnapping by Dark Mafia."* Prior to his own persecution, Gao conducted numerous investigations into the facts and circumstances behind the persecution of Falun Gong practitioners under the Chinese Communist Party (CCP), and had exposed his findings to the world in the format of open letters to Chinese leaders. Among the very few people who dared to speak out on the subject of Falun Gong's persecution, Gao is one of the earliest and most courageous. As indicated above, his words are painful and his descriptions shocking. To be honest, I have had to stop reading on several occasions. How I wished the facts in Gao's account were not true and I could just turn away and return to my comfortable, seemingly controlled existence. Yet, this was a reality I felt I could not ignore. A person's ability to withstand torture is limited. As T. S. Eliot once said, "Humans cannot bear very much reality."

In retaliation of Falun Gong and in order to force practitioners to renounce their faith, the CCP's repression and torture of Falun Gong have reached the point of unscrupulousness. For the last 15 years, the well-ordered machine of the persecution, from the directives of the CCP's highest leader to the lowly ranking personnel who carry out orders, Falun Gong practitioners face a huge human rights disaster. Before the persecution began on July 20, 1999, up to 100 million people were practicing Falun Gong, according to the government's own estimates.

It has become an unwritten rule that Falun Gong practitioners killed by the *"610 Office"*—an agency created solely for the purpose of persecuting Falun Gong practitioners, and those who participate in the persecution of Falun Gong, are not subject to legal action. Moreover, arbitrarily kidnapping and detaining Falun

Gong practitioners are not subject to any restriction or penalty. According to the Minghui website, a confirmed total of 3,795 Falun Gong practitioners have been persecuted to death as of November 2014, the actual number is estimated to be much higher. Gleaned from the large amount of reports with unbearably heartbreaking details of the slaughter, the atrocities can be compared to those at Auschwitz—where 1.1 million people perished. In 2007, David Kilgour, a former Canadian Secretary of State for the Asia Pacific region and former member of Parliament, together with David Matas, Canada's international human rights lawyer, conducted an independent investigation and arrived at the conclusion that "there has been and continues today to be large scale organ seizures from unwilling Falun Gong practitioners." Moreover, the researchers noted that organ harvesting is happening in many Chinese provinces simultaneously. They described China's crime of organ harvesting in China as "an unprecedented evil on this planet."

I do not intend to go into any descriptive reiterations of the tragedies to which Falun Gong practitioners are subjected, as the facts can easily be found on the internet. Rather, my intention in this essay is to examine the world's terrible silence in the face of these horrendous acts of violence.

Two: Experiencing the impassable in the silence

In China, people keep silent about the Falun Gong issue as if nothing is happening. On the internet, searches on any information of Falun Gong come up empty, and there is hardly any discussion on this topic in any microblog or micro-channel. No reporter will take a second to consider investigating or reporting news about Falun Gong, whether it is about one person being kidnapped or 100 people being killed. Intellectuals and pundits will not consider writing on this topic; scholars will not incorporate the facts of the persecution in their academic research. The vast majority of lawyers shun Falun Gong cases, and the self-proclaimed "Die Hard Lawyers" likewise refuse to represent Falun Gong. Even democratically-minded people, dissidents, and human rights workers never mention the Falun Gong issue, as if it has no relation to human rights.

The situation outside China is not much better. The mainstream media do not want to report news about Falun Gong. Politicians do not speak about Falun Gong. Writers do not write about Falun Gong. Scholars do not do research on Falun Gong. Even a considerable number of human rights organizations are reluctant to talk about Falun Gong.

Could it be that they do not know the truth? The problem may not be they do not know, but rather they do not want to know. The 1999 nationwide campaign-style crackdown descended on Falun Gong in a frenzy, utilizing the entire nation's propaganda and media machines to criticize and demonize Falun Gong with trumped up lies such as the staged event of self-immolation in Tiananmen Square, false reports that Falun Gong teachings forbid practitioners to seek medical treatment, and that practitioners have threatened the government, etc. The propaganda was and has been insidious; pervading all organizations and corporations as well as elementary schools and universities. I remember at the time I was working on my PhD at Peking University where every student had to submit a written report on their personal understanding of Falun Gong. Xu Zhiyong, another PhD student, and I attended a symposium where representatives from many Beijing universities and those from the liberal arts community were also in attendance. At the symposium, only Xu Zhiyong and I raised the subject regarding the government's violation of the "rule of law" in their treatment of Falun Gong. Nobody else responded or made any comment whatsoever.

Even though information on Falun Gong has met with the most rigorous ongoing blockade by the Great Firewall of China (GFW), Falun Gong practitioners have invented a variety of easy-to-use software to break through the GFW. So, it is impossible for people who have the capability to "scale the wall" not to have come into contact with such information. Network administrators responsible for reviewing the networks would have been notified that terms such as "Falun Gong," "Li Hongzhi" (founder of Falun Gong) and "live organ harvesting," are all sensitive terms. Lawyers would have been notified that Falun Gong cases are sensitive cases. In fact, even without these notifications, people would instinctively know that these terms and topics are off limits. According to the "spiral of silence" theory, everyone has a "quasi-statistical organ" similar to the "sixth sense," so that even without public opinion polls, people still know what is overwhelmingly mainstream public opinion. As social beings, we fear isolation and will often avoid any activities that are likely to lead to disconnection. Highly sensitive topics including Tibet, the Uyghur conflict in Xinjiang, the corruption of Chinese officials, China's black jails and the June 4th student massacre, are topics the Chinese people and many outside of China will not publicly address. At the top of the list is the persecution of Falun Gong. People know what happened to Gao Zhisheng, Li Hong, Wang Yonghang, and Liu Ruping. People know their classmates or neighbors who practice Falun Gong are kidnapped time and time again or later die mysteriously at brainwashing centers. People know that speaking up for Falun Gong will likely result in not being able to obtain a passport, losing employment, and even being sent to force labor camps or simply disappearing. People know that the wisest and safest approach is *don't look, don't listen, don't speak.*

Three: Turning the silence

The shocking reality of the persecution is the elephant in the room; no one wants to deal with it. In his 2007 book, *The Elephant in the Room: Silence and Denial on Everyday Life*, Eviatar Zerubavel explains this as a matter of "We know but realize that we are supposed not to know." This is similar to what George Orwell referred to as "doublethink", in *1984*. In a state of helplessness, where people feel that they do not have the power to change what needs to be changed, people are well aware that certain things which cannot be adequately addressed should remain private. People understand that Falun Gong is something the Chinese authorities do not want people to know about, and will go to any lengths to silence those who speak out. So the Chinese people know these words well: *"Don't say. Don't look. Don't ask. Don't get curious."*

The Chinese people know that the persecution of Falun Gong is in itself too abysmal a topic to address. In 2007, when I was working on Wang Bo's case, I came to appreciate how deeply disturbing this issue truly is. Inside and outside the courtroom, the air was filled with hostility and tension. After the court hearing, I was carried off by four bailiffs and thrown outside the Shijiazhuang courthouse. The street was heavily guarded, in dead silence. Such an atmosphere of terror was significantly stronger than when I had previously worked on any other human rights case. It can easily be imagined how the authorities were shocked and angry when we published on the internet our well-researched defense pleas that "constitution is supreme, faith is guiltless." These defense pleas completely negated the legitimacy of the Chinese authorities for persecuting Falun Gong and exposed the crimes of the Chinese authorities for brutally trampling on religious freedom.

It takes courage to face the truth, and this is true for those in and outside of China. Journalist Ethan Gutmann's book *The Slaughter: Mass Killings, Organ Harvesting and China's Secret Solution to Its Dissident Problem* exposes, in great detail, the truth about the persecution of Falun Gong. Jay Nordlinger, senior editor of the National Review, acknowledges his difficulties in reading Guttmann's book: "[I] confess to skipping some pages and turning away from photos...." I remember to this day my similar reactions upon reading Gao Zhisheng's candid and unsettling account: anxiety, depression, panic, and an attempt to deny what I read.

The persecution of Falun Gong is beyond human imagination. The details of the torture and of the cruelty exercised by the evil perpetrators are too horrible, far exceeding what most of us can accept. Our initial first reaction is invariably skepticism. Reports out of the early Soviet Union, Nordlinger writes, were dismissed as "rumors...[t]ales of the Holocaust were Jewish whining." The possibility of such horrors is frightening.

This is a critical moment in our shared consciousness. To accept the horrors committed by the CCP, we want to regard such events as isolated and not recognize them as the massive crimes that they are. How else can we manage to deal with circumstances that we believe are beyond our control?

Yet, the only way for the persecution of Falun Gong to end is for any of us to face up to this extreme evil and extreme suffering. We cannot say that this is a rare occurrence in our history. We must acknowledge the seriousness of the government's crimes, give these crimes their rightful attention and consider the implications of these crimes. Having endured tremendous mental or emotional shock, our hearts and spirit will become stronger. The crimes of the CCP and the suffering of its people will not cease to exist because we ignore them. On the contrary, our disregard is exactly the prerequisite needed for the perpetrators' arrogance.

Sometimes, we just need to listen to our inner voice, or reflect on things around us with a little curiosity. A friend once told me a story: after graduating from his university, he went from Shandong to Guangdong to look for work. The work unit asked him to provide documents of verification that he had no criminal record and had never practiced Falun Gong. These documents were mandatory for obtaining a passport and for job applications. He had never heard of Falun Gong until then, and didn't understand why it was necessary to have such proof, so he "scaled the wall" and learned about the government's persecution of Falun Gong.

But to reveal publicly what one knows is not easy. There is the risk that this seemingly simple moral act will not only incite persecution at the hands of the authorities, but will also result in tremendous pressure from the visible and invisible "silent majority." Exposing the truth will shed light on the government's crimes and in doing so may interfere with the vested interests of certain parties; highlight the immorality of those who remain silent; and disrupt the safe and sweet rhythm of life that people hope to maintain. We like what is comfortable and controllable: "Chicken Soup for the Soul," sweet lullabies, and films with a happy ending. We don't like blood and tears, suffering and having to consider the finality that death brings. But, the more we face what is uncomfortable, the more precious our courage, and the more significant and impactful our truth telling becomes for all of humanity. In places where silence is prevalent, in an era of rampant tyranny and lies, exposing the truth is not only the beginning of resistance, but is precisely what lies at the cornerstone of healing and change.

Four: Dismantling the reverse causality

It is human nature to often view difference in others with apathy or even disdain. With the help of state run media, Falun Gong practitioners in China are treated as enemies, cultists, lunatics and preposterous. These views are entertained in order to alleviate the psychological pressure of the evildoers and reduce the moral responsibility of the silent masses. Some even blame Falun Gong practitioners for the persecution! This kind of reverse causality equates to holding the unarmed students and citizens responsible for the Tiananmen Square massacre.

Using the media and its power to influence the international community, the CCP has manipulated how people in and outside of China view the nation. Consequently, people are awed by China's magnificent skyscrapers and superhighways, rising incomes among a formerly impoverished population, the dexterity and skill of the nation's Olympic gold medalists and the government's pretenses of honoring traditional culture through the many Confucius Institutes sprouting up around the world. The sensitive topics are, for the government, conveniently dismissed or misunderstood.

While the CCP, including the originator of the persecution, former head of the Chinese government Jiang Zemin and Zhou Yongkang, once a top official in the CCP and the *610 Office*, obviously hold primary responsibility for the persecution of Falun Gong, the world's silence, this shameful co-conspiracy— bears the same inescapable moral responsibility. Without the hundreds of millions of people to participate in this "conspiracy of silence," it would be almost impossible for the Falun Gong issue to not become the biggest elephant in the world.

Elie Wiesel said Auschwitz is "not only a political reality, but also a cultural fact," and above all, it is "the vertex of irrational contempt and hatred."

The same is true with the persecution of Falun Gong. The facts of the Nazi Holocaust have been revealed to the world, the perpetrators have been punished, and people have given this episode of our shared history an invaluable amount of recognition and appreciation. Yet, the barbaric actions of the CCP, with the medieval forms of torture and the concentration camps reminiscent of the Nazi era are still rampant in today's China. Falun Gong's persecution continues, the perpetrators remain at large, and violence persists. Too many of us turn a blind eye and a deaf ear, failing to understand that our silence and indifference leads us to act as conspirators of these outrageous atrocities! We must remember that we pay the price for our actions as well as our inactions. The words of Martin Luther King Jr. act as an important reminder: "The day we see the truth and cease to speak is the day we begin to die."

The Viciously Toxic Economy of "Red" Capitalism in Communist China

By Wu Hui-lin, Ph.D.

A "Harmonious society" is a society filled with happiness. Even the leaders of the Chinese Communist Party (CCP) know that. To create a harmonious society thus becomes the common objective for policy makers. Then, what exactly is a harmonious society?

The Real Meaning of a Harmonious Society

The word for "harmony" in Chinese is written as "和諧." The character "和" includes the character for food, "禾," and the character for mouth,"口," suggesting that there is food available for every mouth. The character "諧" includes the character for speech, "言," and the character for all,"皆," suggesting that everyone has freedom of speech. In order for everyone to have enough food, it is necessary to implement a "free economy, a private property economy or market economy." In order for people to have freedom of speech, a "free democratic system" is the prerequisite.

After almost 100 years of communism, we have no evidence that this system of government has contributed to a harmonious society, and it has to progress to "economic freedom" and "political freedom." The next question is: do we need to implement both at the same time, or one after another? Since the former will cause trauma in a short time, the latter was used more often. Then which one should be implemented first: "economic freedom" or "political freedom?" Creating material wealth, after all, is a much simpler and better manageable prospect than developing programs to further and sustain human rights. Therefore, many governments tend to implement economic freedom first and then practice democracy. Yet, choosing to expand the economy does very little for strengthening a harmonious society, so progress tends to be slow. The CCP of course, follows the "economy first" model, so democracy is far below what one would expect from the second largest economy in the world. The world is not lacking of successful cases such as Taiwan and Chile.

It was well known that by implementing the policy of "decentralization of power and transfer of profits" at the end of 1978, then-premiere of the CCP Deng Xiaoping, along with leaders of the Soviet Union and various Eastern European countries, tried to transform state-owned properties into private ownership. At the beginning, the policy was successful and Zhao Ziyang, China's third premiere under CCP leadership, was the true person behind the wheel. Before rising through the ranks to act as premiere of the Party, Zhao was the Secretary of the Party Committee in Sichuan Province in 1975. At that time, the lives in Chinese villages were quite impoverished due to the Cultural Revolution. Zhao hence adopted the "ease of restriction" policy, which allowed peasants to freely plant commercial crops, renewed the policy to allow household sideline production, allowed them to have their own land to grow crops for their own consumption and promoted the reform policy of "the privatization of farm output quotas for individual households." Motivated by these incentives, the peasants worked hard and Sichuan enjoyed several years of prosperous harvests. Because his economic reforms were so successful, Zhao was acknowledged by Deng Xiaoping and other leaders, and was accordingly appointed as Premiere in the early 1980s.

Along with then-Communist Party General Secretary Hu Yao-bang, who was also well-known for his liberal style, the two formed the so called "Hu-Zhao system" under Deng's leadership, and vigorously promoted agendas for both economic and political reform. Generally speaking, Zhao was in charge of economic reform, and applied what he had learned from his achievements in Sichuan to the whole country.

The dilemma of Zhao Ziyang's economic reform

In short, Zhao's reform was intended to achieve privatization. However, it would prove to be neither an easy nor quick process. Zhao had to make a choice: either promote the ideological agenda of his stakeholders, the Party, or resist their pressure and meet the needs of the people. In addition, despite Zhao's recent accomplishments in Sichuan, his limited experience—he only received a high school education and never lived beyond the restrictions of a communist state—caused people to doubt his capability in fulfilling such an enormous task. However, on the afternoon of September 19, 1988, after a decade of economic reform in China, Zhao had a two-hour conversation with Noble laureate and liberal economist Milton Friedman (1912-2006), on the topic of "the issue of economic reform in China." It was indeed surprising to know that after the conversation, the well-known Chinese economist Steve Cheung commented that both Zhao and Friedman shared a "similar" point of view.

Cheung's observation is illustrated in a "Christmas letter," the only one written by Friedman and his wife to one of their relatives in more than a decade. In this letter, Friedman described Zhao as: "We are very impressed with Zhao's wisdom and his leadership in bringing China to a more market oriented economy. He has a very deep understanding about the economic issues, is determined to expand the market [and is] willing to try and learn. He is humble and sincerely listens to recommendations and comments from others. In the meantime, he also has to safeguard the highest authority of the CCP. If he is to succeed, this requires very subtle tactics. At the moment, he is facing some real problems, mainly that the acceleration of inflation will slow down the pace of economic reform."

Accordingly, the economic reform implemented by Zhao was indeed effective in the early stages. However, as his goal to safeguard the highest authority of the CCP conflicted with that of an expanding market, it was inevitable that he would be faced with a serious dilemma. In addition, Cheung worried that the economic reform would lead China toward the Indian-like "classified management" that occurred in the early stages of Indian reform. As expected, the reform ended up in that direction. Although Zhao was under house arrest after the 1989 Tiananmen incident, his approach of progressive economic reform, combined with maintaining the highest authority of the CCP, was still followed by the CCP. As a result, conflicts finally happened and the situations of "institutional corruption" and "curse to the late comers" plainly appeared in China.

"June 4th, 1989" and "April 25th, 1999": two turning points of democratization in China

The "June 4th student massacre" of 1989 was a turning point for China's transition to democracy. Unfortunately Zhao, who firmly believed in the CCP's internal reform, dared not challenge the student suppression, orchestrated by such leaders as Deng Xiaoping, Li Peng, and Jiang Zemin. Instead, with tears in his eyes, he persuaded students on Tiananmen Square to cease their protests.

Shortly afterwards, army tanks rolled in without any hesitation, leaving behind the bloody bodies of innocent students. Zhao was later purged and put under house arrest. The democratization attempts in China ended in vain.

The "June 4th Incident" sparked global outrage, with countries worldwide adopting economic sanctions against China. The nation's economy, already in an impasse because of monetary failures, plummeted to dangerous levels. Due to economic stagnation, the unemployment rate kept increasing and social unrest continued to escalate.

In 1992, the spiritual, self-cultivation system Falun Gong (also known as Falun Dafa) was introduced to the public. With its easy to learn gentle exercises and emphasis on improving one's moral character, the practice had attracted 100 million adherents within a few short years. Falun Dafa, an ancient form of qigong, teaches practitioners to first look inward when encountering conflicts and to practice the principles of truthfulness, compassion, and tolerance to transform hostility into harmony.

With one in 12 Chinese people improving themselves through Falun Dafa, many social problems throughout the country, resulting primarily from unemployment, easily dissolved. For several years, the Chinese government praised the benefits of Falun Dafa for improving social well-being, but their position gradually turned more hostile before the official crackdown on July 20, 1999.

On April 25, 1999, about 10,000 Falun Dafa practitioners from all over China gathered at Zhongnanhai, the government compound in Beijing, to appeal to the central government for justice for their fellow practitioners who had been detained and the recent defamation of the practice. With a calm mindset and respectful behavior, they held a peaceful, quiet appeal that is unprecedented in Chinese history.

Then-Premier Zhu Rongji met with Falun Dafa representatives during their protest and gave them a reasonable response to their complaints. Afterwards, the practitioners left in an orderly manner without leaving a single scrap of litter on the assembly site.

CNN and every other foreign media present at the scene were stunned by the peaceful demeanor of the practitioners and offered high praise for their efforts. Journalists reported that it was the largest group of demonstrators in China since the 1989 student protests and recognized the gathering as a pivotal moment in furthering democracy in China. Leaders of many foreign governments and those in the legal and political fields also considered the demonstration a model for China's responsiveness to its citizens; a second chance for the CCP's reform towards liberal democracy. However, subsequent developments deeply disappointed the international community.

Suppression of Falun Gong brings serious disaster

Three months after the April 25 peaceful appeal, the CCP initiated the "bloody repression against Falun Gong" on July 20, 1999, sabotaging any possibility for a harmonious society. To persecute Falun Gong practitioners, the CCP established the *610 Office* and spent a lot of money to force police and all citizens in China to report Falun Gong practitioners. Practitioners were subject to arrest, imprisonment, torture and to having their organs forcibly harvested. In addition, to cover up the facts of its bloody suppression, the CCP has not only monitored media and built up a strong cyber army to defame and slander Falun Gong but also offered economic bribes in exchange for Western politicians' silence. To support the abundant resources needed for the suppression, the CCP had to retain a high GDP growth with minimal production costs.

The consequences of the government's misdeeds include the following:

1. Escalation of sweatshops appearing throughout China.

2. Cheap consumer goods, which have contributed to global deflation.

3. Considerable consumption of natural resources by Chinese production, raising the price of electricity and other resources, leading to "imported inflation."

4. Domestic and international inflation, due to depressed export prices of Chinese goods so that the government can acquire huge amounts of foreign exchange; such depression also creates a money bubble with manipulative financial risk, which can induce global financial disasters.

5. Emergence of environmental crisis, air pollution, and poisonous haze as natural resources are exhausted.

6. Low quality and even poisonous products sold locally and exported to foreign countries, resulting in illness, injury, and even death.

7. Human rights are neglected as foreign policy makers are intentionally distracted by China's financial incentives.

8. Chinese society is increasingly corrupted as morality declines and people are led by greed and the desire for personal gain.

The negative impacts of China's high growth rates have prompted serious concern among experts in a variety of different fields since the beginning of the new millennium. Leaving aside the authenticity of these economic figures, the high growth rate in a totalitarian state is achieved by consuming and wasting natural resources. Paul Krugman, the recipient of the 2008 Nobel Prize in Economic Sciences, clearly pointed out in his article "The Myth of Asia's Miracle" published by *Foreign Affairs* in 1994, that speedy economic growth in communist countries is based on an increase of input rather than the increase of *output-per-unit-of-input*. Such actions will eventually lead to diminishing returns and slowed growth by a wide margin. Hence, since the year 2000, the economic development in China has been described as "outwardly strong but inwardly weak," "a castle in the air," "a rotten interior beneath a fine exterior," and "about to collapse."

It is well known that the CCP is skilled in the manipulation of human resources. As the government has narrowly pursued economic growth in China, Chinese workers are exploited and their salaries are depressed. The consequence of which is worldwide "deflation" (overproduction, low prices, and poor quality). Other countries, being dissatisfied with China's tactics, take actions to boycott, retaliate, and even riot against the CCP. An example was the furious public burning of Chinese shoes in September of 2004 in Spain.

Cheap and adulterated goods are poisoning ordinary people

> "A farmer bought plump rice seeds and planted them. However, nothing grew out of those seeds because they were fake seeds. The angry farmer tried to kill himself by taking poison. But he did not die because the poison was bogus. His wife bought wine to celebrate his survival. However, they both lost their lives because the wine was poisonous."

The above joke was circulating on the internet.... Of course, China's maltreatment of human resources and cheap, defective products is no joke. Economically robust countries around the world, including the U.S., are threatened by low-priced goods made in China. In the quarterly issue of *Journal of Economic Perspectives* in September 2004, P. A. Samuelson (1915-2009), the recipient of the 1970 Nobel Prize in Economic Sciences, coined the term "polemical untruth" to denounce outsourcing production, widely recognized at the time as a useful option in promoting growth. Cheap goods such as "shoes Made in China," he noted, are the result of outsourcing and negatively impact the employment of low-level workers in the US.

It is understandable if Chinese workers, of their free will and informed consent, voluntarily compromise their well-being to labor under poor working conditions while earning low wages. The Chinese government, however, is an authoritarian regime which is not ruled by law but by party guidelines. The majority of its workers have no choice but to be exploited. For instance, the Lanzhou Zhenglin Farming Foods Company, established and funded by Taiwanese enterprises in 1992, exported its "exclusively created AAA grade hand-selected large melon seeds" to many countries. The melon seeds were produced by about ten thousand detainees who were forced to crack melon seeds with their teeth and open them with their bare hands. The detainees were not paid. In winter, their hands succumb to frost-bite and scabies. As they labored without any medical care, blood dripped from their hands onto the melon seeds. Their teeth and nails were destroyed (EpochTimes report on September 13, 2004).

Following the reports of defective China-made tires, toothpastes, and toy trains, a New York Times report on June 29, 2007, listed five types of seafood (catfish, sea bass, shrimp, dace, and eel) which were found to contain harmful antibiotics and were included in the list of poisonous goods by the U.S. It is worth noting that these reports are not just isolated incidents but have continued to surface around the globe, one after the other. Many reports from Western media have observed that China, as the world's production factory, poses serious threats to global health.

When will the catastrophe of global resource depletion end?

Before the public was made aware of China's poisonous products, the government's emerging economy garnered positive praise from almost every corner of the globe. A few warnings did appear but were ignored. The more China's growth rate grew, the more local and international markets consumed; the government made sure demand was met no matter the environmental or human consequences. Social inequity and distress in Chinese society—problems once hidden to the international community—have become increasingly serious and blatantly obvious as reports of slave workers emerge and the disparity between rich and poor becomes more extreme. The CCP has used its financial power as a means of coercion and inducement in exchange for advanced technological products, forcing some companies like Yahoo! to assist the CCP in conducting domestic surveillance. As a result, free speech, human rights, and political freedom in China have worsened. Moreover, the CCP's bribes to silence foreign politicians has resulted in the entire international community remaining mute in the face of the CCP's human rights violations. Some have even become accomplices.

The impact of China's rapid growth on the global environment and natural resources has attracted attention from all over the world. A report by the Greenpeace organization on October 19, 2005, pointed out that China has become the largest contributor to the destruction of rainforests: "Nearly five out of ten tropical hardwood logs" from the world's threatened rainforests were being shipped to China that year. In addition to causing global deforestation, China's demands for grain, meat, iron, and coal have exceeded that of the U.S., making China the world's largest consumer. It will not end until we quickly change the mode of development in China. Without doing so, the disasters in the world will be extensive and devastating.

In addition to the export industry, large-scale infrastructure, i.e., construction projects, throughout China consume even greater amounts of resources. Such projects are vehicles for collusion—and potentially corruption—between the private and the public sectors. While China moves forward with these massive projects to build its GDP, the supply and investment excess and the enormous demand shortage of their actions have created serious problems which will inevitably contribute to huge unaffordable debt and idle buildings.

By developing its economy at the expense of precious resources, the CCP has led the world to a critical point. The naked reality of *diminishing returns* has occurred in the wake of the competition for resources between China and other countries. The economic growth of China will be decreased deeply in the near future, which will harm both the Chinese people and the rest of us. Hence, for the sake of all humankind, we sincerely hope for an immediate change of China's economic development model. Only through democracy, freedom, and open markets can we be saved.

In conclusion, the CCP must disintegrate, China's red capitalism must become a pure market economy, and China must become a democratic country. Otherwise human disasters will escalate and destruction of civil societies will be inevitable.

Section III

MEDICINE

Unprecedented Evil Behind Forced Organ Harvesting: The Choice to Die Spiritually or Physically

By Torsten Trey, M.D., Ph.D.

Unprecedented evil and an absurd medical practice

People everywhere embrace human dignity, basic freedoms and the right to live peacefully. The medical profession is dedicated to serving human beings in recovering from illness and, if successful, in helping to prolong life. This is the mission of the medical profession. The medical oath speaks of doing no harm. Thus, it is appalling that the medical profession in China is taking part in ending the lives of prisoners of conscience for the purpose of harvesting and transplanting their organs. It is both, transplantation for profit and a method of persecution.

A Chinese law, passed in 1984, permitted organ harvesting from prisoners, but it was only after 1999 that transplantation in China soared significantly. Where did the transplant organs come from? After millions of spiritual believers and members of ethnic groups became subject to dehumanization, ostracism and persecution, the 1984-conditioning of harvesting organs from executed prisoners expanded to an even larger pool of organ sources— prisoners of conscience. In short, transplant medicine in China became an absurd medical discipline; it is incomprehensible to provide health care to one group of people by forcibly ending the lives of another group.

Since 2006, investigative reports and other published evidence pointed out that prisoners of conscience, particularly adherents of the persecuted spiritual discipline Falun Gong, were subject to forced organ harvesting. Within five years, three books on the subject were published discussing the issue from various angles: *Bloody Harvest* (2009), State Organs (2012) and *The Slaughter* (2014). Investigators compiled compelling, although mostly circumstantial evidence. Yet, since July 2006, after the first publication of the Kilgour and Matas report (that resulted in *Bloody Harvest* three years later), no international inspection of Chinese transplant centers has taken place. To date, China has failed to respond to the body of evidence in an adequate manner.

Instead, the *China Medical Tribune*[1] from November 2014 quotes Professor He Xiaoshun at a press conference, discussing the demand for further investigation with Professor and former deputy health minister of China Huang Jiefu, "Let us open the doors, and let the international scholars come to investigate these rumors [about unethical organ harvesting]." Professor Huang replied, "It is not time yet." If it is not time yet, when will it be time? What are they waiting for?

Attempts to deceive

On June 27, 2001, Chinese surgeon Wang Guoqi testified before the Subcommittee on International Operations and Human Rights of the United States House of Representatives that in China organs were harvested from prisoners after execution.[2] On June 29, 2001, the *New York Times* quoted China's Foreign Ministry spokeswoman, Zhang Qiyue, saying that Dr. Wang's testimony was "sensational lies," and "a vicious slander" against China.

"The major source of human organs comes from voluntary donations from Chinese citizens," she said.

In 2006, The *Guardian* reported that Huang, in December of the previous year in Manila, "made the first official admission that the country harvested organs from executed prisoners."[3] In November 2006, Huang reiterated in Guangzhou that most of the transplant organs came from executed prisoners, except for a small number of traffic accident victims, thereby completely contradicting Zhang's early statement.

In 2007, one year before the Beijing Olympic Games, at the annual General Assembly of the World Medical Association (WMA) in Copenhagen, the WMA announced an agreement with the Chinese Medical Association (CMA). The CMA stated that "organs of prisoners and other individuals in custody must not be used for transplantation, except for members of their immediate family."[4] In a letter to the WMA, Vice President and Secretary General of the CMA, Dr. Wu Mingjiang said:

> "A consensus has been reached... that organs of prisoners and other individuals in custody must not be used for transplantation, except for members of their immediate family."

Yet, after 2007, the transplant numbers were reported to remain as high as 10,000 per year. In 2012, the Washington Post quoted the Chinese health ministry stating that "10,000 organ transplant operations are performed annually," and that 65% of those transplants are performed with organs from executed prisoners. It is unlikely that all the tens of thousands of transplant patients after 2007 were "members of the immediate family" of executed prisoners.

In 2009, The Telegraph quoted Huang saying death row inmates were "definitely not a proper source for organ transplants."[5] On May 17, 2013, an Associated Press article quotes Huang at a Beijing conference, saying that the organ procurement from executed prisoners is "profit-driven, unethical and violating human rights."[6] But three days later, when asked about using prisoners as an organ source in an interview with *Australian ABC TV* on May 20, Huang stated:

> *"Why do you object? I have no objections to using the executed prisoners' organ donation if he or she has freely demonstrated that this is his last will."* [7]

In March 2012, Huang said that China will establish an organ donation program and promised to end the government's reliance on executed prisoners' organs within three to five years. [8]

Eight months later, in November 2012, Huang said, "China will end its reliance on executed prisoners' organs in one to two years."[9] Then in March 2014, Huang stated, "executed prisoners are also citizens. We cannot deny their rights to donate organs," indicating that China will continue to use organs from prisoners. He also stated that, once the executed prisoners are entered into the China Organ Transplant Response System (COTRS) as citizen donations, there would be only one concept, namely citizen donation.[10]

Between 2001 and 2014, Chinese officials repeatedly made contradictory statements on the sourcing of transplant organs. This flip-flopping has misled and deceived the international community, making it quite clear that China's assurances are unreliable. In this context, Huang's comment that it is "not time yet" is not surprising. China is buying time.

China's flip-flopping is not a coincidence. It is intentional. It causes confusion, distracts from the underreported organ harvesting from prisoners of conscience and prevents the international community from seeking outside investigations and inspections of Chinese hospitals. Any delay in demanding international inspections results in the delay of what our professional responsibility demands: ending this horrendous medical abuse. Our delay comes at the cost of human lives. There is no doubt that Western organizations and officials have certainly demonstrated patience, but the past 14 years of micro-actions after Dr. Wang's testimony are paved with more than 150,000 transplant organs sourced from a more or less equal amount of convicted prisoners and prisoners of conscience.

To die spiritually by being forced to sacrifice one's belief, or to die physically by being forced to sacrifice one's life for transplant is a stark reality for Falun Gong practitioners in China. While the perpetrators give their victims the choice to die either spiritually or physically, the people in the free world have the choice to act or to ignore. The *transplant cannibalism* in today's China is unprecedented in known history and requires unprecedented actions.

One such action was the founding of the medical NGO, Doctors Against Forced Organ Harvesting (DAFOH). DAFOH focuses on a niche topic within the field of transplant medicine: forced organ harvesting without free, voluntary consent. Yet, the underlying issue, the intentionally induced death of "organ donors," shakes the foundation of medicine and must not stay unanswered by the medical community.

The call to end the killing for organs is not interfering with internal state affairs—it is a moral obligation.

In a country where verdicts are known to be decided before a court case opens, where defense lawyers are prohibited from defending death row candidates, and where courts approve of organ harvesting after executions, there is no rule of law. Consequently, if we are to be completely frank in addressing China's practices, the terminology "organ procurement after execution" should be replaced with "state sanctioned killing for organs." It is our moral obligation to call for an end to transplant medicine that is taking part in such abuses.

The exponential increase of transplant numbers within four years after the onset of the persecution against Falun Gong is noteworthy. Why did the practice become subject to this abuse? Falun Gong practitioners aspire to improve their moral character by following the universal principles of truthfulness, compassion and tolerance. After July 1999, they became subject to brainwashing, forced labor and torture. Death by torture of Falun Gong practitioners is widespread in China.

A few moments of browsing the website *www.faluninfo. net* provides insights into the extent of the brutality of the persecution. The basic problem is that once respect for human beings is lost, and the right to live and the right to believe is refused, nothing remains. From the perpetrator's side, there is literally no difference between death by torture and killing prisoners of conscience for their organs, except that, in the latter case one can turn the bodies of tens of thousands of prisoners of conscience into a profit of several billion dollars.

With the Kilgour and Matas report in 2006, China's unthinkable crime lost its cover. The investigations of the past years have generated persuasive pieces of evidence, with each piece like a piece of a puzzle. And, like a puzzle, the more pieces that are in place, the more visible the picture and what were once only allegations are now shown as irrefutable facts. Refusing to recognize the picture because the last five or ten puzzle pieces are missing is equivalent to ignorance. The initial Kilgour and

Matas report carried 17 pieces of evidence, three years later, their book *Bloody Harvest* (2009), carried more than 50 pieces of evidence. Additional reports and published works with new evidence have followed in the years since while the response from China has remained evasive. Instead of simply proving the allegations wrong by allowing for international inspections, an array of announcements and promises have served to distract the public. The government's measures of deception succeeded in preventing the international community from calling for inspections of Chinese hospitals and detention camps.

Pilot research by DAFOH in 2014 looked into the phenomenon of widespread medical exams from Falun Gong practitioners in China's forced labor camps. Those camps, by their very nature, exploit forced labor without paying adequate salaries. Yet, according to the number of testimonies collected in the study, it is would appear that tens of thousands of costly medical exams have been imposed primarily on Falun Gong practitioners detained in forced labor camps.[11] The medical exams were forced upon the practitioners, who did not ask for or agree to it. Instead, it was routine to take blood from inmates when they arrived in the labor camps. These blood tests, urine tests, x-rays, ultra-sonograms, etc., are costly. If the wellbeing of the inmates was of concern, why not simply provide fresh food and water, clean restrooms and less than 17 hours a day of forced labor? Amortization of the medical expenses through transplants would certainly balance the costs and help to provide a sufficient amount of organs.

Why is Falun Gong being persecuted without adherents of the practice having violated any laws and without having done any harm? The reason for the persecution and its subsequent forced organ harvesting comes down to the principles of goodness for which the practice stands: truthfulness, compassion, forbearance, which lie in direct opposition to Communist Party ideology:

- While Falun Gong aspires to truthfulness, the agenda of the Chinese Communist Party (CCP) is based on biased information, propaganda and deception.

- While one side aspires to goodness and compassion, the other side preaches class warfare, expropriates farmland and rules with an iron fist.

- While one is tolerant, the other punishes anyone who has an opinion or thought other than the Party's guidelines.

The only aspect of civil disobedience of Falun Gong practitioners in China lies in the wish to freely believe in truthfulness, compassion and tolerance, and freely practice a set of five gentle, qigong-like exercises. Outside China, this is not considered civil disobedience but a precious, laudable contribution to society. In this regard, to answer the question why Falun Gong is persecuted in China and subject to forced organ harvesting, one might look to Henry David Thoreau:

> *"Under a government which imprisons any unjustly, the true place for a just man is also a prison."* [12]

Under the totalitarian regime in China, where the rule of law does not exist and court sentences are decided before a hearing begins, we are more likely to find just people in prisons. Falun Gong carries the most valuable principles for humankind and has, since 1992, irrefutably done more for human dignity and the good of mankind than the CCP. The government's hatred of Falun Gong and other kind-hearted freethinkers is neither a problem of Falun Gong nor a problem of the people. It is a problem that the CCP has with mankind. The Chinese regime gives detained Falun Gong practitioners a choice: recant your free belief or suffer. This is also the choice that the CCP gives to the people of the world.

Killing people for their organs contradicts everything for which humankind and the medical profession stand.

When human life and universal principles are at stake, speaking up and calling for an end to forced organ harvesting is not only a basic right, but a moral obligation. Calling for an end to forced organ harvesting of Falun Gong practitioners and other prisoners of conscience requires calling for an end to the persecution. Human dignity and basic rights do not terminate at a country's borders. By definition they are inherent in mankind. China's assertion that discussing human rights is interfering with the country's internal affairs is blatant hypocrisy: by suppressing basic human rights and global initiatives to improve quality of life, the Chinese regime has interfered with the internal affairs of the world's people and their nations.

Calling for an end to forced organ harvesting of Falun Gong practitioners and other prisoners of conscience is the basic right of all people, and the Chinese government should refrain from interfering in the internal affairs of the world's people. The persecution against Falun Gong and its three principles is a persecution against goodness in mankind. The driving force behind China's forced organ harvesting is unprecedented in its evilness and necessitates an unprecedented, determined action from humankind. It is a choice of life.

[1] http://www.cmt.com.cn/detail/623923.html&usg=ALkJrhj1Ume7SWS_04UtatL3pWKYRbFxqw (last accessed Nov 21, 2014)

[2] http://waysandmeans.house.gov/legacy/trade/107cong/7-10-01/7-10wolf.htm (last accessed Nov 12, 2014)

[3] http://www.theguardian.com/world/2006/apr/19/china.health (last accessed Nov 12, 2014)

[4] Peter O'Neil; China's doctors signal retreat on organ harvest; Canadian Medical Association Journal; 2007 November 20; 177(11): 1341. http://www.ncbi.nlm.nih.gov/pmc/articles/PMC2072972/ (last accessed Nov 12, 2014)

[5] http://www.telegraph.co.uk/news/worldnews/asia/china/6094228/China-admits-organs-removed-from-prisoners-for-transplants.html (last accessed Nov 12, 2014)

[6] http://bigstory.ap.org/article/cultural-attitudes-impede-organ-donations-china (last accessed Nov 12, 2014)

[7] http://www.abc.net.au/news/2013-05-20/chinese-doctor-hits-back-at-critics-over-organ-donation-program/4701436 (last accessed Nov 12, 2014)

[8] http://news.qq.com/a/20120322/001592.htm (last accessed Nov 12, 2014)

[9] http://finance.chinanews.com/jk/2012/11-21/4347626.shtml (last accessed Nov 12, 2014)

[10] http://news.sciencenet.cn/htmlnews/2014/3/289619.shtm (last accessed Nov 12, 2014)

[11] http://www.dafoh.org/implausible-medical-examinations-falun-gong-forced-labor-camp-workers/ (last accessed Nov 12, 2014)

[12] Henry Thoreau, Civil Disobedience and Other Essays; http://www.brainyquote.com/quotes/quotes/h/henrydavid135750.html (last accessed Nov 12, 2014)

China's Execution-Transplantation System and International Institutions: A Too-Sticky Wicket?

By Kirk C. Allison, M.S., Ph.D.

Introduction

The nexus of transplantation and execution in China and professional association responses highlight tensions between disciplinary standards and self-regulation. While not wholly autonomous, characteristics justifying professions' unique legal standing include specialized expertise, self-regulation (practice standards and discipline), and serving the public interest including protecting "against bungling and extortion."[1] Thus, "it alone must exercise discipline over its members, and with due regard to basic human rights, remove delinquents from its lists."[2] What response should follow when an entire context of professional practice shows no regard to basic human rights, even relying on execution for its materials?

The Case

After years of denial, in 2005, Vice Minister of Health and liver transplant surgeon Huang Jiefu admitted executees were China's primary organ source.[3] The confluence of Falun Gong persecution, launched in 1999, and an exponential increase in organs with a peak in 2004 (see Fig. 1) [4] has had little acknowledgment in professional society discourse, despite increasing recognition among medical professionals and ethicists.[5][6]

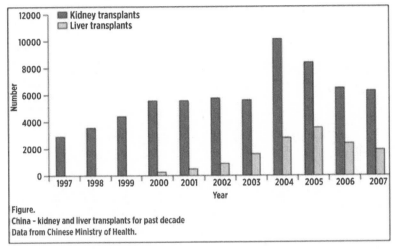

Figure.
China - kidney and liver transplants for past decade
Data from Chinese Ministry of Health.

Fig. 1

Professor Shi Bingyi (Transplantation Director, 309th People's Liberation Army Hospital Beijing), stated transplants peaked at 20,000 in one year—2006, not 2004, thus if accurate contradicting MOH presented data.[7]

Evidence of Falun Gong sources has led to European Parliament Resolution 2013/2981, (December 2013),[8] and, with 215 cosponsors, House Resolution 281 has been approved unanimously by the U.S. House Committee on Foreign Affairs in July 2014, "Expressing concern over persistent and credible reports of systematic, state-sanctioned organ harvesting from non-consenting prisoners of conscience, in the People's Republic of China, including from large numbers of Falun Gong practitioners imprisoned for their religious beliefs and members of other religious and ethnic minority groups."[9]

The pattern characterizes a supply-driven market, not merely capacity increase; a supply glut processed down (2004-2005), servicing the lucrative transplant tourist flow.[10] In 2005, the China International Transplantation Network Assistance Center's homepage boasted: "Viscera providers can be found immediately!"[11] Whence such 'providers'?

Liver transplants lagged kidney, negligible before 2000 (< 350), peaking in 2005 (3,500+), before dropping in 2006 below 2004 levels. This reflects numerous hospitals entering the more lucrative liver transplant market after the kidney peak. By 2006, 500+ Chinese hospitals performed liver transplants, compared to about 100 in the U.S.[12]

Hao Wang's 2007 time-series study (data 1993-2005) indicates confirmed Falun Gong detention death trends (2,773 between 1999-2005) predict liver transplant trends highly significantly ($t=10.16$, $p<.00001$), while Chinese media execution reports did not ($t=0.57$, $p=.5792$). The study points beyond the official explanation of judicial executions being the main source of the 'surplus' organ explosion. *Non gratas* tortured to death have little transplant value; however, a Falun Gong practitioner refusing to recant or identify him/her self in detention could generate several hundred thousand dollars. Preparatory examinations (blood draws, x-rays, etc.) are multiply attested.[13] In 2006, 120 calls to hospitals and 36 to detention centers and courts yielded 19 acknowledgements of available Falun Gong organs. Many skirted the sourcing question as a sensitive secret.[14]

Co-Responsibilities

Given disciplinary and commercial cognizance of China's execution-transplantation system, this chapter examines two institutional documents and material supporting services:

- The Transplantation Society member letter of November 6, 2006 (hereafter "member letter").[15]

- Declaration of Istanbul on Organ Trafficking and Transplant Tourism (2008).[16]

- Pharmaceutical and diagnostic interests and supports.

Beside China's vacillating ethical self-assessments, execution-based transplantation has been termed unethical, immoral, evil, barbaric or genocidal depending on context. International transplant societies' primary strategy has been mostly 'constructive engagement', not isolation. Are those efforts or actions by market seekers licit or complicit? Has proximity to China enabled continuance?

Cooperation in evil? A heuristic framework

While terms of opprobrium are fitting, a more differentiating structure may clarify proximity and culpability: *cooperation in evil* (borrowing a Catholic taxonomy). One may use another term than *"evil"* however which will indicate the gravity accorded to what is at stake.

Cooperation concerns an act, here procuring/transplanting executee organs. The agent performs; cooperators assist. Either may be personal or institutional. Cooperation devolves at three levels: intentional (Formal) or practical (Material) cooperation; the nature of material support (Immediate or Mediate); and the level of proximity to the act (Proximate or Remote).[17]

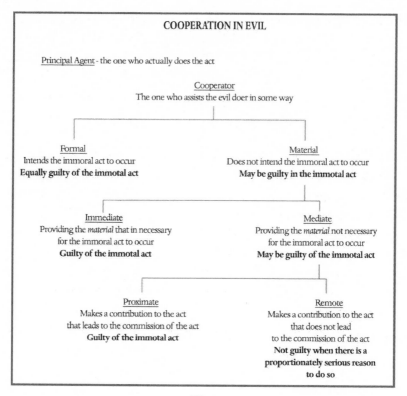

Fig. 2

Formal cooperation concerns intent (transplant tourist approving source). *Immediate material* cooperation involves an integral contribution necessary for the act (training). *Mediate* contributions are involved contextually, but not integrally. *Proximate* ones may *lead* to the act (agreeing to attend an academic transplant demonstration); a *remote* one does not per se (selling surgical drapes to a hospital). One could triply intend, provide necessary material, and proximately contribute. Unless an act is intrinsically evil, context is determining. Hence a good in one context (transplantation) may represent an evil in another (execution-transplantation). Intent, an act's moral nature, and consequences are each in play.

In China, physicians, (i.e., principal agents) co-effect execution in transplant selection and scheduling[18][19] (if not taking organs alive), raising the question whether organ availability is a 'byproduct' (aftermarket, value-added) or prisoners are executed *for* organs.

The Transplantation Society member letter of November 6, 2006 — generating change through proximity?

The Transplantation Society (TTS) is a "NGO in official relations with the World Health Organization—WHO."[20] *Transplantation*, the official journal, "the most cited and influential journal in the field" with a vision to "provide the focus for global leadership in transplantation" in "development of the science and clinical practice," "scientific communication," "continuing education," and "guidance on the ethical practice." TTS boasts 6500+ members in 100+ countries and a biennial congress of 5,000+ participants.

On November 6, 2006, TTS issued a 3-page member letter on China and other countries not conforming to its Policy & Ethics or Membership statements. It announced work with WHO and Chinese government agencies, "to develop a legal framework that achieves TTS standards of practice" and WHO guiding principles.[21] For this, "interaction with Chinese officials is the only true route to effect long term change" and "must be derived from Chinese Governmental policies;" suggesting other routes would be 'false'. Further, TTS endorsed a recent MOH statement of "new ethical standards."

Before 2006, no centralized oversight was attempted; a well-connected military medical system outside the MOH drove the lucrative transplant tourist boom (*bing shang* – soldiers in business) with few organs for ordinary Chinese. A decentralized death penalty system allowed broad discretion with 68 capital crimes as did seasonal "strike hard" campaigns until capital punishment review returned to Beijing in November, 2005. Capital crimes reduced to 55 in 2011, with reduction to 46 proposed in 2014.[22]

The TTS member letter presents four "realities and principles"; 1) China's prominence (11,000+ transplants in 2005). 2) "Almost all organs are likely to have been obtained from executed prisoners." 3) "As a professional society, TTS cannot dictate to China that its practice regarding capital punishment is unethical" — despite the documented arbitrary nature. Rather, "TTS should express concern that recovery of organs from executed prisoners has resulted in rampant commercialism and transplant tourism." 4) MOH intent to create national oversight, establish credentials, ban organ commerce, prevent trafficking/tourism, establish deceased donation (brain death criteria) and self-sufficiency with deceased and living donors. Strongly emphasizing unlikelihood of free consent by prisoners, "financial incentive for recovering organs from executed prisoners may become an incentive to increase the number of such organs available for transplantation."

For China the letter welcomes TTS membership for anyone signing the membership statement; TTS meeting attendees can include personnel transplanting executee organs (for dialogue/promoting alternatives); scientific presentations from China not involving executees and research collaborations, when IRB/Helsinki Declaration-compliant, welcome. Member lectures and expertise may support China's program if, "as far as possible," not promoting executee use; and international registries may accept duly noted executee sourced transplant data for transparency/demographics, but not aggregate outcome reporting.

By 2005, China International Transplant Network Assistance Center attributed its capacity almost entirely to Western training (eleven surgeons and two physicians).[23] Astonishingly the TTS letter encourages Western institutions to accept new transplantation trainees from executee-using programs, if ensuring, "as far as possible," intent to follow TTS guidelines in the future. Some institutions, however, took a radically different tact: In December 2006, transplant centers in Queensland, Australia, banned further training of Chinese surgeons and related joint research.[24]

While TTS intends no executee use (no 'formal cooperation in evil' nor complicity in membership or registry tracking, if compliant), research discussions provide mediate support on return to China; meeting contents (new techniques) make integral contributions; and new training increases capacity for any organ source.

Did the TTS member letter's approach work? — Seven years later, (February 27, 2014) TTS and the Declaration of Istanbul Custodian Group published an *Open Letter to Xi Jinping President of China, President of the People's Republic of China: China's Fight against Corruption in Organ Transplantation.*[25] Advocating "a culture of human rights," urging Xi to address still ongoing unethical transplant practices, "to rid Chinese society of corruption," including coerced consent, "notorious transactions between transplant surgeons and local judicial and penal officials," "clandestine organ transplants," and continuing transplant tourist marketing; in sum, "decades long malpractice." Among the standards cited is the 2008 *Declaration of Istanbul on Organ Trafficking and Transplant Tourism.*

The Declaration of Istanbul on Organ Trafficking and Transplant Tourism

April 30 - May 2, 2008, a Summit convened in Istanbul to "assemble a final declaration that could achieve consensus" on organ trafficking and transplant tourism. A Steering Committee (TTS and International Society of Nephrology leadership) provided a working draft. Some 170 invited potential participants represented diverse countries and interests; 160 participants accepted (four from China) and 152 attended. A worksheet assigned PRC participants to Governing Principles and Communication Plan and MOH representative Zhao Minggang to *Transplant Tourism*.[26]

Declaration Principle six addressed organ trafficking/transplant tourism, referencing World Health Assembly (WHA) Resolution 44.25 *Human Organ Transplantation* (1991).[27]

Principle 6a) calls for advertising, soliciting and brokering bans; 6b) for penalties for related screening, transplanting, and acts "that aid, encourage, or use the products of, organ trafficking or transplant tourism." Pharmaceuticals or other supports are unmentioned save acknowledging Summit funding from Astellas Pharmaceuticals — the major supplier of anti-rejection drugs in China.

Principle 6c) broaches prisoners, first and last …

> *"Practices that induce vulnerable individuals or groups (such as illiterate and impoverished persons, undocumented immigrants, prisoners, and political or economic refugees) to become living donors are incompatible with the aim of combating organ trafficking, transplant tourism, and transplant commercialism."*

… only as living donors, not executees (unless killed by organ removal). By April 2008, all Summit participants knew China's ongoing organ source: hundreds of executees monthly. Was mentioning this considered unnecessary given reform promises or blocked by China's representatives?[28]

In 2008, TTS awarded Huang Jiefu its *President's International Award* for "the favorable changes and good progress in the regulatory development related to organ transplantation in China ..."[29] Surprisingly, at the end of 2008, Vice Minister of Health Huang, responsible for organ procurement practices on the civilian side, still cited executee sourcing at 90%.[30]

The Declaration of Istanbul Custodian Group (DICG) was established in 2010 to promote Declaration principles; participants and organizers subsequently spoke out on China's ongoing execution-transplantation reality.[31] Yet the Declaration's silence — *unregistered as a category of concern* — remains a remarkable event in disciplinary self-censorship.

Supporting Services and Vested Interests

Each TTS webpage acknowledges four corporate sponsors: Japan-based Astellas Pharma, U.S.-based One Lambda (Thermo Fisher Scientific), Swiss-based Roche, and Paris-based Sanofi. Each has significant involvements in China not indifferent to TTS policies.

Astellas Pharma

Astellas Pharma China, Inc. notes use of immunosuppressive Prograf® (tacrolimus) to prevent liver and kidney graft rejection in China since 1999.[32] This predates Wang Guoqi's 2001 landmark Congressional testimony on organ harvesting, including from still living executees. The webpage identifies tacrolimus use in China in over 20,000 cases and 20 million worldwide, China patients comprising 0.1%. Not surprisingly, www.astellas.com.cn fails to mention that physicians prescribing and patients receiving Prograf® rely chiefly on executee organs.

Astellas commenced drug trials in China statistically requiring executees after the TTS member letter; March 2007 (42 livers), July 2007 (240 kidneys) and January 2008 (172 livers).[33] Prograf® study site, First People's Hospital (Shanghai) acknowledged Falun

Gong sources on March 3, 2006.[34]

In 2011, prominent ethicists and transplant surgeons declared, "Time for a boycott of Chinese science and medicine pertaining to organ transplantation"[35] noting "pharmaceutical companies continue their marketing efforts and engage in sponsoring research involving various aspects of transplantation in China." In 2011 Astellas introduced Advagraf® to the PRC ("New Prograf extended release capsules").[36] Despite well-known execution-transplantation, Astellas aims for monopoly claiming "application of other immunosuppressive drugs cannot control graft rejection."[37]

Immunosuppressive therapy is downstream from selecting and killing prisoners, yet without this, fewer near matches would be used. In 1999, Astellas was likely unaware, but now expanding in such a system is culpable. Astellas could declare a moratorium date and exert significant pressure rather than continuing cooperation. Immunosuppressive therapy is not integrally tied to execution, but supporting the organs-through-execution market is.

Whether a company foreswears a lucrative market position may come down to public exposure and what company leadership, and shareholders, can stomach after recognition.

Roche

Roche began anti-rejection drug trials in China during April, 2006; 36 hearts, 90 livers and by September, 2008, 210 kidneys.[38] On March 16, 2006, one Roche trial involved Shanghai Jiaotong University Hospital's Liver Transplant Centre, where a Dr. Dai identified organs available within a week, including Falun Gong sources.[39]

In September 2009, Arne Schwarz queried a Roche compliance

officer. The response: "Roche is, as mentioned above, neither in China nor in any other country of the world in charge of the supply of organs. Anonymity and privacy of the most highly personal donor data are protected by law. Roche is not entitled to know from where or from which donors the transplanted organs come."[40] Transplant journals now require executee-free source certification, why not Roche? Where the vast majority of organs are sourced unethically, corporate responsibilities cannot hide behind a foil of respecting anonymity and privacy. Here, both serve complicity with a lethal system and endanger prisoners of conscience, chiefly, but not limited to, Falun Gong.

In 2010, Roche rightly received two unwanted "Public Eye Awards" in Davos, Switzerland, for Cell Cept® trials, without verifying organ sources.

One Lambda (Thermo Fisher Scientific)

One Lambda is a world leader in HLA tissue typing, HLA antibody detection, transplant monitoring and diagnostic products. Acquired in 2012, such "complement our existing immunosuppressant assays, which are used to monitor the level of drugs in transplant patients," an opportunity to accelerate growth faster than U.S. rates.[41] Roche's 2012 *Annual Report* reflects $700M China sales (up 22%), primarily lab consumables well aligned with China's Five-Year Plan.[42]

Sanofi

In 2013, Paris-based Sanofi celebrated 30 years in China with a new 3.5B capacity pill plant in Hangzhou.[43] In 2009, it had China's first international biotech R&D hub.[44] Acquiring Genzyme Corp., Sanofi entered the transplantation field in April 2011, including an "immune-suppressive and immune-modulating agent that aids in the prevention and treatment of acute rejection." It also distributes antithymocyte globulin against bone marrow rejection. The China Bone Marrow Donor Program and database are under the Red Cross Society of China. Prisoner sourcing has not yet been identified.[45]

The cooperation/complicity analysis of TTS sponsors is left as an exercise for the reader.

Conclusion

The intersections of China's execution-transplantation system with the persecution of Falun Gong; professional and commercial responses, responsibilities, and contradictions, while reflection on the nature of culpable cooperation even in the midst of well-meaning engagements, invite several conclusions and a more effective response.

For professions to foreswear the legitimacy of their practice is difficult even in unethical (in this case homicidal) contexts, particularly when promoting an intrinsic good (i.e., health); likewise for companies to give up expanding markets given ethical contraindications.

TTS acknowledges no prima facie right to an organ. A few licit sources do not redeem the majority of illicit ones. 'Constructive engagement' has been selectively accepted by China, resulting in an increase of capacity (training surgeons) and unimpeded continuation also after the use of prisoners organs were admitted to by hospitals surgeons and detention centers.

In summer 2005, law professor Qu Xinjiu (Political Science and Law University, Beijing) addressed China's "transplantation bank" pointing out lack of consent and danger that health officials' organ demand would influence sentencing. He called for immediate moratorium.[46]

Prudence is the virtue of attaining morally laudable ends by morally consonant means. There is no prudent path to an immoral end nor prudent complicity in immoral means. Both China's medical establishment and population are addicted to sourcing organs from prisoners, including prisoners of conscience.

Ending even indirect support of a lethal organ procurement system is likely the most efficient path to the good while avoiding complicity; compelling populace, politicians and medical functionaries to make a choice.

In 2013, Huang, et al. errantly stated, "the need of the Chinese people for high-quality organ transplant services is our obligatory mission."[47] If China's population does not highly value transplantation, with their own organs voluntarily in the game, no transplant would be the logical, ethically obligatory consequence.

Formerly Vice Minister Huang called prisoner sourcing "variously improper, unethical, violating standards, and vulnerable to death penalty reform." In a 2014 China Times interview he offers instead a final, but only semantic solution:

> *"Executed prisoners can voluntarily donate organs. Given the willingness of death row prisoners to donate organs, once entered into our unified allocation system they are counted as voluntary citizens – the so-called death row organ donation doesn't exist any longer."*[48]

Here the China Organ Transplant Response System (COTRS) performs as immediate efficient sanitizer. China's medical system and population continue to rely on execution; physicians codetermine execution; Western institutions enable continuance. All except prisoners, especially prisoners of conscience, have a choice.

COTRS Director Wang Haibo: "The question is, indeed, when can China solve the deficit in donor organs? I wished we could stop with that tomorrow. But it requires a process. Many things evade our control. Therefore we cannot name any timetable."[49] Clearly, it is well past the time for Western entities to stop enabling and align action with moral responsibilities.

[1] Klass, A.A., "What is a profession?" Canadian Medical Association Journal, 85(1961):698-701.

[2] Klass, p. 699.

[3] Following Chinese: family name, given name.

[4] Huang J, Mao Y, Millis JM. "Government policy and organ transplantation in China," Lancet 372(2008):1937-1938.

[5] Caplan A.L., "Polluted sources: Trafficking, selling and the use of executed prisoners to obtain organs for transplantation." In: Matas, D. and T. Trey (eds.) State Organs (Woodstock ON: Seraphim, 2012), pp. 27-34.

[6] Sharif A., M. Fiatarone Singh, T. Trey, and J. Lavee. "Organ procurement from executed prisoners in China." American Journal of Transplantation 14,10(2014):2246-2252.

[7] Xu, Y. 供体短缺是制约器官移植事业发展的瓶颈 ("Donor shortage is a bottleneck restricting the development of organ transplantation"). Science Times, 6/15/2007. http://paper.sciencenet.cn/html/showsbnews1. aspx?id=182075. Comparative graphs: http://www.stoporganharvesting.org/quantity-skyrocketed.

[8] European Parliament resolution of 12 December 2013 on organ harvesting in China. (2013/2981(RSP)) http://www.europarl.europa.eu/sides/getDoc. do?type=TA&reference=P7-TA-2013-0603&language=EN&ring=P7-RC-2013-0562.

[9] H.Res.281 – 113th Congress (2013-2014). https://www.congress.gov/bill/113th-congress/house-resolution/281.

[10] Wang, H. "China's Organ Transplant Industry and Falun Gong Organ Harvesting: An Economic Analysis." Thesis. Yale University, 2007. See pp. 16-18. http://organharvestinvestigation.net/events/YALE0407.pdf. Also Gutmann E. The Slaughter: Mass Killings, Organ Harvesting and China's Secret Solution to its Dissident Problem (New York: Prometheus Books, 2014), pp. 217-253.

[11] China International Transplantation Network Assistance Center, "Introduction to China International Transplantation Network Assistance Center." ©2004-2005. http://en.zoukiishoku.com. (Website down. Author's screenshot available.)

[12] Zhang Feng, "New rule to regulate organ transplants." China Daily, 5/5/2006. http://www.chinadaily.com.cn/china/2006-05/05/content_582847.htm.

[13] Gutmann, pp. 29, 186-187, 233-237, 239-240 (also 'Eastern Lightning' Christians), 244 (Tibetan monk report), 282 (Uighurs), 320-321 (16 of 50 FG interviewees in Thailand recounting exams). 364 (indexing exam types).

[14] Matas D. and D. Kilgour. Bloody Harvest: The killing of Falun Gong for their organs (Woodstock, ON: Seraphim Editions, 2009), pp. 80-93 (example transcripts).

[15] The Transplantation Society. "To TTS members," 11/6/2006. [No longer on TTS website.] http://transplantation.graydesign.com.au/files/StatementMembs-ChineseTXProg.pdf

[16] "The Declaration of Istanbul on Organ Trafficking and Transplant Tourism." Clinical Journal of the American Society of Nephrology, 3(2008):1227-1231.

[17] Archdiocese of Philadelphia. "Cooperation in Evil" [chart]. s.d. http://archphila.org/HHS/pdf/CoopEvilChart.pdf. Typo edited.

[18] Selection lists identified by transplant tourist spouse, execution timing triggered by matching. Kilgour and Matas, 62-63.

[19] Laogai Research Foundation, Involuntary Donors: A Comprehensive Report on the Practice of Using Organs of Executed Prisoners for Transplant

in China (January 2104), pp. 119-120. The report, however, does not remark on evidence of Falun Gong and other prisoners of conscience as sources.

[20] The Transplantation Society. "About TTS." http://www.tts.org/about-tts-5.

[21] Letterhead lists TTS President/Historian Nicholas L. Tilney; Director of Medical Affairs Francis L. Delmonico. Ethics Committee under Annika Tibell composed the guidelines also for consideration by Global Alliance for Transplantation organizations.

[22] AP. "China considers ending death penalty for 9 crimes," 10/29/2014. http://bigstory.ap.org/article/1c1950e80db54763ab82232d88ee7cd8/china-considers-ending-death-penalty-9-crimes.

[23] Listed: University of Nebraska, Emory, Toronto, Hong Kong, Hanoverian University, Minnesota, Tokyo, Kumamoto, Queensland and Flinder Center. China International Transplantation Network Assistance Center, "Introduction to Doctors." http://en.zoukiishoku.com/list/doctors.htm. Update 7/20/2006. Website down. Author's screenshot available.

[24] "Hospitals ban Chinese surgeon training." Sydney Morning Herald, 12/5/2006.   http://www.smh.com.au/news/National/Hospitals-ban-Chinese-surgeon-training/2006/12/05/1165080933418.html.

[25] The Transplantation Society & Declaration of Istanbul Custodian Group, "Open Letter to President of China," 2/27/14. https://www.tts.org/home-660/newletters/past-newletters/2014-volume-11-issue-1/1585-open-letter-to-president-of-china.

[26] Istanbul Confirmed Groups April 8.xls.

[27] See related resolutions at http://www.who.int/transplantation/publications/en.

[28] "The content of the Declaration is derived from the consensus that was reached by the participants at the Summit in the plenary sessions." Clinical Journal of the American Society of Nephrology, 3 (2008):1230.

[29] Kuhn, R.L. How China's Leaders Think (Singapore: Wiley and Sons (Asia), 2010), p. 301.

[30] Lancet 372(2008):1937-1938.

[31] See articles at http://www.declarationofistanbul.org/articles/articles-relevant-to-the-declaration.

[32] Astellas, 移植免疫: 普乐可复 (他克莫司胶囊、注射液) ["Transplant Immunology: Prograf (tacrolimus capsules, injection).] http://www.astellas.com.cn/?productshow/pid/197/tp/198/id/2.

[33] Schwarz, A. "Responsibilities of International Pharmaceutical Companies in the Abusive Chinese Organ Transplant System," State Organs, pp. 119-135.

[34] Matas D, "Antirejection Drug Trials and Sales in China," American Society of International Law Annual International Conference on Law, Regulations and Public Policy (LRPP 2012), Hotel Fort Canning, Singapore, July 8 [sic! 9], 2012, pp. 3-5.

[35] Caplan A.L., G. Danovitch, M. Shapiro, J. Lavee, and M. Epstein. [Same title]. Lancet 378(9798):1218. http://www.thelancet.com/journals/lancet/article/PIIS0140-6736%2811%2961536-5/fulltext.

[36] Astellas, 移植免疫: 新普乐可复 (他克莫司缓释胶囊) ["Transplant Immunology: New Prograf (tacrolimus extended release capsules)".] http://www.astellas.com.cn/?productshow/pid/197/tp/198/id/3.

[37] 治疗肝脏和肾脏移植术后应用其他免疫抑制药物无法控制的移植物排斥反应。http://www.astellas.com.cn/?productshow/pid/197/tp/198/id/2.

[38] Schwarz, p. 123.

[39] Matas D, "Antirejection Drug Trials and Sales in China," American Society of International Law Annual International Conference on Law, Regulations and Public Policy (LRPP 2012), Hotel Fort Canning, Singapore, July 8 [sic! 9], 2012, pp. 3-5.

[40] Schwarz, pp. 124-125. My trans. per German, 113n25.

[41] Thomson Reuters Street Events. "TMO – Thermo Fisher to Acquire One Lambda Conference Call," 7/16/2012. http://ir.thermofisher.com/files/events/2012/TMO-Transcript-2012-07-16.pdf

[42] Thermo Fisher Scientific. 2012 Annual Report, p. 3.

[43] Sanofi. "Annual Review 2013: Protecting Life, Giving Hope." http://www.sanofi.co.za/l/za/en/layout.jsp?scat=86ABAAB0-44B1-4769-8D9A-

6BA1C270B3C5.

[44] Pharmaceutical-technology.com. "Genzyme R&D Facility, China," s.d. http://www.pharmaceutical-technology.com/projects/genzyme-facility/

[45] China Marrow Donor Program (CMDP). http://www.cmdp.com.cn/cmdpboard.do?method=showEnglish&parentId=7.

[46] Stock, O. "Transplantationsbank China: Warm Roche mit seinem Anti-immunmittel Erfolg haben wird," Handelsblatt,11/7/2005. http://www.handelsblatt.com/unternehmen/industrie/warum-roche-mit-seinem-anti-immunmittel-erfolg-haben-wird-transplantationsbank-china/2572842.html .

[47] Huang, J., S.-S. Zheng, L. Yong-Feng, H.-B. Wang, J. Chapman, P. O'Connell, M. Millis, J. Fung, and F. Delmonico. "China organ donation and transplantation update: the Hangzhou Resolution." Hepatobiliary Pancreatic Dis. Int. 13,2(2014):122-124.

[48] Sharif, Fiatarone Singh, Trey, and Lavee, p. 4; Dailynews.sina.com. 黄洁夫：内地已有38家医院停用死囚器　[Huang Jiefu: Mainland has 38 hospitals stop using prisoner organs.] 3/4/2014. http://dailynews.sina.com/gb/chn/chnpolitics/phoenixtv/20140304/12205515629.html.

[49] Kirchner, R. "Keine Organe mehr von Hingerichteten?" Tageschau, 4/14/2014. http://www.tagesschau.de/ausland/china2158.html.

URLs accessed 11/24/2014.

Forced Live Organ Harvesting— Transplant Abuse by the Chinese Communist Party

By Dr. Huang Shiwei

1. The Case

In September 2003, a 35-year-old male hemodialysis patient went to China for a kidney transplant. He had already completed tissue matching and other preoperative evaluations in Taiwan, and was informed that there was a HLA 3 matching kidney available. He was on his way to the First People's Hospital affiliated with the Shanghai Jiaotong University in China. However, upon a final cross matching test, it was discovered that the reaction was positive and the kidney was unsuitable. In order to avoid hyperacute rejection (an event that occurs minutes after transplantation and can result in organ failure within hours), he was asked to wait for a new organ. In the next two weeks, three matching kidneys were found and brought to hospital accompanied with a tube for cross-matching test, but they all tested positive. The three kidneys were discarded. At that time, the patient had to return to Taiwan as he only had three weeks sick leave from work.

In March 2004, the patient had a long vacation and decided to go back to the Shanghai First People's Hospital for kidney transplant. His doctor in Taiwan told him that another HLA 5 matching kidney was available. However, the cross-matching reaction was still positive again. The doctor in China advised him to undergo plasmapheresis (a process used to filter blood and remove harmful antibodies) while the doctor in Taiwan advised him to continue to wait. He waited for another three weeks. A fourth kidney finally showed a negative cross-match. He successfully underwent the transplant surgery. A week later, he began his rehabilitation at the ward for overseas Chinese at the People's Liberation Army 85 Hospital. The entire medical and travel expenses he spent was about 28,000 US dollars. The patient said the doctor in China told him the kidney was secretly taken from an executed criminal. He also said that when he had become flustered during the wait, that same doctor had comforted him by showing him multiple sheets of (more than 20) consolidated donor information and telling him there were many highly suitable donors among the list so that all he needed to do was continue to wait. He further indicated that patients from Korea, Japan, and Malaysia as well as mainland China came there for organ transplantation.

2. The broker who introduced the patient to a hospital in Guangdong Province for kidney transplant

Between 2000 and 2006, the Chinese organ market witnessed an excess supply over demand. It rarely took more than a week to find a match. The doctor in that hospital is solely responsible for performing transplant surgeries. The transplant surgeon only needs to "place the order" and someone delivers the requested organ, or a hospital worker takes an ice bucket to get the organ. Before 2006, a doctor only needed to pay a "higher authority" 600 US dollars (not including bribe money) to obtain an organ. The broker for these transplant procedures was made to believe that this higher authority was the court. A broker told the following story: One time, a hospital worker transported eight kidneys by air. Because of a snowstorm and subsequent flight delays, he arrived late at the hospital. Upon examination, the doctors determined that the kidneys were not qualified for transplantation. They ordered the replacements and informed the eight patients that they had to hold off for a few more days for a new batch of kidneys. The broker knew that HLA 3 matching is a minimal requirement. He had seen detailed information about the donors in a doctor's computer. He thought that China has a repository supply of organs from executed prisoners, and that the time of execution was in line with the need of organ transplantations. All brokers know that only military doctors have access to the organs. Patients would go to military hospitals or the transplant departments in domestic hospitals run by military doctors to receive transplantation surgeries. Although many foreigners come for organ transplantations, transplant recipients are mainly Chinese. The cost for a kidney transplant is only about 8,000 U.S. dollars. In addition to low cost for high quality organs, the hospital, as we confirmed, boasts short waiting periods, with transplantations having a high success rate. China is a country that lacks comprehensive medical insurance. When organ transplantation is cheaper than dialysis, Chinese prefer organ transplantation over dialysis due to the lower cost. With regard to livers: In China, liver transplantations are in high demand due to a high incidence of hepatitis B.

3. Hospitals in Mainland China

The Shenyang City International Transplant Network Support Center[1] was set up in the First Affiliated Hospital of the China Medical University in 2003 as an organ transplant website to attract foreigners. The hospital's website reports that the Chinese government has made it possible to perform a large number of transplantation surgeries. The law jointly declared by the Chinese Communist Party's (CCP) Supreme People's Court of the People's

Republic of China, Supreme People's Procuratorate, Ministry of Public Security, Ministry of Justice, Ministry of Health and the Public Ministry[2], states that organ supply is supported by the Chinese government. This is unheard of in any other countries. The question and answer section of the website promises that the quality of the organs is guaranteed by the use of "living organs," rather than organs procured from brain-dead patients or from patients whose hearts have already stopped beating:

> "**Question**: Are pancreas transplant organs from brain-dead patients?
>
> **Answer**: Our organs do not come from brain-dead patients, because the condition of these organs may not be good.
>
> **Question**: Even if the transplant is successful, the postoperative survival time is no more than two to three years, right?
>
> **Answer**: This type of question has been asked a lot. The short survival time refers to Japan where they took kidneys from the brain dead donors. In China, we have kidneys from living donors. It's completely different from Japanese hospitals and dialysis centers because they conduct kidney transplants from dead donors."

In addition, the hospital's website clearly outlined the price for each organ:

$62,000 U.S. dollars for kidney transplantation
$98,000 to $130,000 U.S. dollars for liver transplantation
$130,000 to $160,000 U.S. dollars for heart transplantation
$150,000 to $170,000 U.S. dollars for lung transplantation

4. Source of organs questionable

With its ability to provide an endless supply of live organs, China has attracted patients from all over the world since 2000. Chinese transplant centers grew from 160 in 1999 to 600 in 2005. The number of transplants rose from 3,000 cases a year in 1998 to nearly 20,000 cases a year in 2005[3]. Patients from South Korea, Taiwan, Hong Kong, Japan, Southeast Asia, the Middle East, Europe and the United States have all flocked to China for organ transplants. However, foreigners only comprise a small portion of organ recipients while the vast majority is from China. Yet China lacks a substantial organ donation distribution system. It thus begs the question—where do these organs come from?

Prior to 2006, Taiwan's main dispute over organ transplantation in China was not the source of organs, but the organ harvesting method. Although many Taiwanese doctors have managed to establish a good relationship with their counterparts in the mainland, doctors from China have never been willing to share information regarding their country's process of organ harvesting with Taiwanese doctors. Chinese doctors indicate that the process of harvesting the organs is a prohibited domain for doctors from Taiwan; the former acknowledge that the organ removal process is very cruel. They openly disclose that the organs they harvest are not from donors who are brain dead or without a heartbeat, but from living donors. They report that most of these organs are removed after the donors are given an injection. What kind of injection do they give to these living donors? On the website, the hospital boasts better quality through living organs rather than brain dead organs. Obviously, this is not only a violation of the "dead donor rule," but also inhumane. Coinciding with their claim, we noted that delayed graft function (a form of renal failure) indeed becomes very rare clinically, reflecting a better acceptance when organs from living donors are used.

In January 2013, a surgeon from Xinjiang Province, China, testified in front of the European Parliament[4]. He talked about his personal experience with the process of organ harvesting and the inmate execution. He said that the executioner would aim the bullet to the right chest of the inmate, wounding but not killing the individual. When the inmate would fall to the ground, the surgeon would then harvest his or her vital organs without anesthesia.

In 2005, former Deputy Health Minister, Huang Jiefu, declared that 95% of organs were from executed prisoners[5]. But, those who understand the Chinese judicial system and the organ allocation provisions[6] know that the death penalty provides two types of execution in China; one is immediate, the other allows a death sentence to be suspended for two years. For the former, the execution must be done within one week after the order is received, which makes it impossible that prisoners sentenced to death can contribute to a standing pool of an available organ supply. In addition, we found that the scheduled surgery for the majority of patients is often one to three weeks after a donor is found, and the date can even be adjusted.

Furthermore, from the medical point of view, death row inmates have a high incidence of drug abuse, smoking, alcoholism, and high prevalence of hepatitis, so it becomes hard to imagine that many good quality organs can be collected only from executed inmates. If death row inmates are not the major source of organs, from where do the majority of China's organs originate? In 1999, General Secretary of the Chinese Communist Party, Jiang Zemin, announced the banning of Falun Gong and carried out his triple policy against Falun Gong practitioners to "defame their reputation, bankrupt them financially, and destroy them physically." The persecution has been utterly brutal. Many have been illegally detained with no formal judicial trial, suffering torture, rape and other forms of maltreatment while incarcerated.

Millions of Falun Gong practitioners have gone missing, with no one knowing their whereabouts.

5. Falun Gong practitioners become the source of organs

It was not until 2006, when two witnesses, Peter, a reporter, and Annie, the ex-wife of a Chinese medical doctor, came forward to allege that the CCP has set up concentration camps to secretly imprison Falun Gong practitioners and harvest their organs for profit[7]. We have to ask how China is capable of providing good quality organs in such large quantities? The answer becomes quite obvious and certain: Good quality organs come from Falun Gong practitioners. David Matas, an international human rights lawyer in Canada, and David Kilgour, the former member of the Parliament and Secretary of State (Asia-Pacific) in Canada, provide more explicit testimonials to this fact in their investigative findings "Report into the Allegations of Organ Harvesting of Falun Gong Practitioners in China"[8].

To this day, faced with the questions and skepticism of the international community, the CCP has still refused any independent and unbiased investigation. Although the CCP promised the international community to reform their organ transplantation system, including terminating the practice of using organs from death row inmates, China's transplant environment remains in violation of basic international norms. The procedures by which it runs its transplant operations are not transparent and the organ source is untraceable. The CCP uses evasive and deceptive language to hide its crimes. Most recently they have revised their transplantation criteria and included death row inmates into their organ allocation system. As a result, death row inmates are now considered citizens who have the right to voluntarily donate their organs.[9] The CCP even planned to transport organs overseas in an attempt to get support from Asian countries.[10] If the CCP truly intends to reform, the government must stop organ harvesting from Falun Gong, and allow independent investigations into the source of each organ of the past 15 years. All perpetrators involved in live organ harvesting must be brought to justice.

6. Conclusion

The Chinese government's program of harvesting organs without free, voluntary consent is an unprecedented evil on this planet. Sadly, it is happening during a time when so many nations around the world are taking human rights as a priority. We have witnessed periods of terrible persecution throughout history, and while these unfortunate events continue across the globe, we have never seen medical doctors systematically engaged in the murder of thousands of innocent lives.

The first time physicians were used on a large-scale to participate in a massacre was during World War II when the Nazi Regime recruited thousands of doctors to participate in the persecution of Jews and other vulnerable people. They conducted despicable experiments, which resulted in disfigurement, permanent disability or even death[11]. Such crimes brought shame to the entire medical profession and eroded public trust in doctors. During the Nuremberg trials, the trial of Nazi doctors was the first of all 12 trials for B class war criminals, indicating the enormous impact that the doctors' involvement had played in these atrocious crimes and the effect their actions had on the global consciousness.

Today, live human organ harvesting in China is a tremendous disgrace to the medical profession and to the entire human race. Organ transplantation is a major medical breakthrough that has saved countless lives over the last century. The CCP, in committing murder for profit in the name of medicine, however, has dishonored the accomplishments of this most vital medical treatment.

Live human organ harvesting is an unimaginable evil in human history. Many simply hope that it is not true or that it is only the actions of a handful of doctors. Facing such brutal facts, many choose to remain silent, either because they find it hard to believe or are swayed by financial interest or reputation. When the evidence is fully exposed, how will we rewrite the history of medicine? How will we justify our silence and give an explanation to the next generation? Chinese people are enduring the largest persecution. If the international community chooses to keep silent, it is the same as siding with evil.

[1] Why was the Chinese web page in the Shenyang Transplant Center deleted;

http://www.epochtimes.com/gb/6/4/6/n1279107.htm

[2] Supreme People's Procuratorate, Supreme People's Public Security Ministry of Civil Affairs Ministry of Justice, Ministry of Health, on the temporary provisions of using bodies of death row inmates or organs from cadavers, October 9, 1984 (84) Division IDRC word No. 447

[3] David Matas & David Kilgour's investigation report on the allegations of the CCP's organ harvesting of Falun Gong practitioners in 2007, revised edition (in English) pp. 40-41 notes 41-45). January 31, 2007

[4] European Parliament hearing focusing on CCP Organ Harvesting;

http://www.xinsheng.net/xs/articles/big5/2013/2/5/49177p.html

[5] Shen Zhengyan. Top official confessed private sale of organs from death row inmates (quoted from British "Times"). Apple Daily (Taiwan). December 4, 2005

[6] Evolution history of organ transplants from death row inmates in Mainland China: Phoenix Weekly | Cover Story | Zhong Jian | 9-24-2013;

http://www.51fenghuang.com/fengmiangushi/2411.html

[7] Sujiatun witnesses exposing the CCP's crime of harvesting organs from living Falun Gong practitioners;

http://www.epochtimes.com/gb/14/4/20/n4135912.htm

[8] Kilgour, David; David Matas. The First Report into Allegations of Organ Harvesting of Falun Gong Practitioners in China. [27 April 2010].

http://organharvestinvestigation.net/report20060706.htm

[9] China to stop using organs from death row inmates on January 1, 2015;

http://news.xinhuanet.com/politics/2014-12/04/c_127278077.htm

[10] Organ platform built between Taiwan and mainland of China. Huang Jiefu: Earliest time for Chinese organs to arrive Taiwan can be next year;

http://www.appledaily.com.tw/realtimenews/article/new/20141219/527018/

[11] Nuremberg "Doctors Trial";

http://www.epochweekly.com/b5/273/10687.htm

Section IV

LAW

Inattention to the Killing of Falun Gong for their Organs

By David Matas

The reaction to the evidence of the killing of Falun Gong for their organs has not been commensurate with the gravity of the offense, nor the quality of the evidence.

Why is this so?

1) Accumulation of evidence

One reason is that going through all relevant evidence—and there is quite a lot of it, to come to an informed conclusion whether Falun Gong are or are not being killed for their organs—is a time consuming task. Many people do not have the time.

Yet, there is no easy short cut. The people present at the scene of organ harvesting of Falun Gong practitioners are either perpetrators or victims. There are no bystanders.

Because the victims are murdered and cremated, there is no body to be found, no autopsy to be conducted. With all but a few exceptions, there are no surviving victims to tell what happened to them. Perpetrators are not inclined to confess publicly, continually and in detail what amount to crimes against humanity.

The scenes of the crimes leave no traces. Once an organ harvesting is completed, the operating room in which it takes place looks like any other empty operating room.

If the story of the killing of Falun Gong for their organs could be told in ten seconds, it would be an easy story to tell. The problem the issue of the killing of Falun Gong for their organs raises is not too little evidence, but rather too much. Because the story is book length, telling it is not so easy.

2) Cover up

The more time passes, the less information is available about transplantation in China and the more sophisticated the cover up becomes. The experience of my research is that as soon as I cite an official Chinese source, it disappears. Advertisements on hospital web sites of short waiting times for transplants have gone, so have public boasts about the amount of money being made from transplants.

Official Chinese price lists for transplants have vanished. Hospitals no longer tell callers that they have organs of Falun Gong within 2-3 weeks for sale.

The liver transplant registry of Hong Kong, which used to post aggregate liver transplant volumes, no longer does. Chinese transplant doctors who used to give referral letters to foreign after care doctors about the operations of their patients data about the organ sources and anti-rejection drugs no longer do so.

The Government of China claims that the prisoners from whom organs are sourced are all prisoners sentenced to death. Yet the Government refuses to release death penalty statistics.

I and others have archived all information we referenced so that independent researchers can see what we saw. However, over time there has been a progressive degradation of the available data from official Chinese sources. There appears to be a systematic cover up of organ sourcing.

3) Newness of the violation

The innovators of transplant technology, we can be confident, never imagined that what they developed would be used to murder prisoners of conscience and sell their organs for huge sums.

U.S. Supreme Court Justice Felix Frankfurter in 1943, reacting to being told by Jan Karski about the Holocaust, Frankfurter said to a Polish diplomat: "I did not say that this young man was lying. I said that I was unable to believe what he told me. There is a difference."

The killing of prisoners of conscience for their organs represents a disgusting form of evil, which, despite all the depravities humanity has seen, is new to this planet. The very horror makes observers reel back in disbelief.

4) Newness of Falun Gong

Repressed democracy activists, journalists, human rights defenders, Tibetan and Christian activists generate more sympathy than the Falun Gong because they are more familiar to the West. The Falun Gong are recent, started in 1992, foreign, without an obvious link to globally entrenched traditions.

To outsiders, there is the immediate albeit superficial strangeness of the name Falun Gong. The words "Falun" and "Gong" in

Western languages mean nothing.

For the Communists, victimizing the Falun Gong is a crime, which is easier to get away with than victimizing other better known groups. Falun Gong victims are often people without Western connections or Western languages. It is a lot easier for outsiders to relate to victims who have universal labels, journalists, human rights defenders, and democracy activists, than a group with a name that means nothing to most ears.

It is much easier to misrepresent the unknown than the known. When the Communists slur Tibetan Buddhists or the Christian house churches, we know that they are talking nonsense. When the Communists slur the Falun Gong, many people are not sure whether there is any basis for the charges.

5) Communist propaganda

Once the Chinese Communist Party/Government decided to ban Falun Gong, the propaganda campaign against the practice of Falun Gong began. This propaganda has been systematic, unrelenting, worldwide. It consists entirely of unfounded stereotypes to justify repression, which exists for entirely different reasons.

The incitement to hatred against the Falun Gong, like all incitement to bigotry, has an impact. The place with the most ferocious impact is China, where the propaganda is uncontradicted. But the incitement has an insidious effect everywhere.

The Chinese noise about the practice of Falun Gong confuses and obscures. Many of those who do not accept in its entirety Chinese propaganda against the Falun Gong, nonetheless, hold the view that there must be something improper about Falun Gong behind all these Chinese charges.

Skepticism about the Falun Gong is not based on anything real in the practice of Falun Gong but is rather the residual impact of the Chinese Government/Communist Party incitement against the practice. Plain and simple, it is prejudice.

6) Contrary interests

China is a global power with economic and political outreach around the planet. China's economic weight by far surpasses that of other major human rights violators.

Some people, for reasons of political or diplomatic or economic convenience, will swallow anything said by the Communist Party of China, true or not. For these fellow travelers, what is relevant is only that it is said by the Communist Party of China. Truth or falsehood is a matter of indifference.

For others, whatever they believe, their sense of prudence dictates silence. They do not want to undercut their own personal interests by saying anything about a matter which does not impact on them personally.

For instance, the Chinese consulate in Toronto wrote city councillors in 2004, urging them to oppose a motion for the proclamation of a Falun Gong week. The letters said: "If passed, the motion will have a very negative effect on our future beneficial exchanges and cooperation." Among the "beneficial exchanges and cooperation" Toronto City Councillor Michael Walker heard mentioned, were threatened sale of a Canadian made nuclear reactor, the CANDU, to China, the construction by the Canadian company Bombardier of a rail link to Tibet, and a two panda loan to the Metro Toronto Zoo[1]. Threats so disproportionate to the event showed the importance to the Chinese Communist regime of silencing the content.

The leverage of the power of the Government of China is particularly evident at western universities. If there is one thing you need to know to understand the Government of China, it is its treatment of the Falun Gong. China treats the Falun Gong as its number one public enemy. China, to all appearances, spends more staff time, money, and effort on the Falun Gong at its embassies and consulates around the world than on anything else. When China fills its prisons and labor camps with Falun Gong, this obsession tells us nothing about the Falun Gong. But it tells us volumes about the Government of China. A focus on Chinese preoccupation with the Falun Gong gives us clearer insights into the mentality and dynamics of the Government of China than any other focus.

Yet, in Chinese studies departments at universities around the world, almost without exception, there are no courses, no research projects, no publications, no guest lectures on the Falun Gong. China studies departments around the world are thunderingly silent about the persecution of the Falun Gong, despite the fact that this persecution tells us more about China than virtually anything else. In China studies departments, the Falun Gong is studiously ignored.

It is as if university physics departments were to ignore Einstein's theory of relativity, as if university English literature departments were to ignore Shakespeare. When universities ignore something so central to China, so obvious, it is not out of ignorance. It is rather out of a desire not to antagonize China. China scholars feel they need cooperation of the Government of China, at the very least to get visas to enter China, to pursue their work. In order to ensure that cooperation, they stay away from a subject the Government of China would not want them to consider. Scholars have enough integrity not to take the Chinese government line on the Falun Gong. But if they say anything else, Chinese officials hit the roof. To avoid that reaction, they say nothing.

7) Lack of structure

Falun Gong is not an organization; it is not even people. It is rather a set of exercises with a spiritual foundation.

The exercises can be done by anyone, anywhere, at any time, though commonly they are done once daily, often together in groups like the many other Tai Chi and Qi Gong practices in Chinese parks. Those who are interested can begin the exercises whenever they want and stop whenever they want. While practicing, they are free to practice the exercises as little or as much as they see fit.

A person need not register with anyone or join anything or pay anything to practice the exercises. All information about how to do the exercises is publicly, freely available.

Those who practice Falun Gong have no organizational leadership. Founder Li Hongzhi is not worshipped by practitioners. Nor does he receive funds from practitioners. He is a private person who meets rarely with practitioners. Most practitioners have never met him.

The lack of structure within the Falun Gong community hampers human rights reporting. There is a website, Minghui, which accumulates reports of victimization. There is also an NGO, the World Organization to Investigate Persecution against the Falun Gong, which does some research and analysis. The website and the NGO are much like the community of Falun Gong practitioners generally, that is to say there is no money, no leadership, no offices, no staff, and a heavy reliance on volunteers.

8) Sympathy for communism

Chinese communists have become so capitalistic, it is surprising to see socialists rallying to the Chinese communist cause. Yet, this phenomenon still exists. The Chinese Communist Party/State has been able to win over to its side many elements of the global leftist community who harbor nostalgia for old time Chinese communism.

This faux leftist solidarity manifests itself in part by rejecting any criticism of Communist China, including criticism of its persecution of Falun Gong. Old time leftists rally around Communist Party fantasies that the CIA is behind Falun Gong[2]. While these sorts of suspicions are too farfetched to get much of a following, they do prevent unanimity across the political spectrum in standing up to the Chinese persecution of Falun Gong in general and the killing of Falun Gong for their organs in particular.

9) Reverse onus

There is an attitude in some quarters that the killing of Falun Gong for their organs has to be established with certainty and, absent that certainty, nothing need be done. This expectation shifts the onus from where it properly lies.

The onus does not fall on researchers to show that Falun Gong practitioners are being killed for their organs. Researchers do not have to explain where China gets its organs for transplants, China does. It falls on the Government of China to explain the sourcing for their organs.

The World Health Organization, in an Assembly in May 2010, endorsed Guiding Principles on Human Cell, Tissue and Organ Transplantation. Two of these guiding principles are traceability and transparency.

At the United Nations Universal Periodic Review Working

Group in February 2009, Canada, Switzerland, United Kingdom, France, Austria and Italy recommended that China publish death penalty statistics. The Government of China said no to this recommendation. The same recommendation was repeated by Belgium, France, New Zealand, Norway, Switzerland, UK, and Italy at the United Nations Universal Periodic Review Working Group in October 2013. This time China said, we'll see.

The connection between death penalty statistics and organ transplant abuse was made explicit by the UN rapporteur on torture, the UN rapporteur on religious intolerance and the UN Committee on Torture. All have asked China to explain the discrepancy between its volume of transplants and its volume of organ sources.

The UN Committee against Torture in its November 2008 concluding observations of the state report of China wrote that China should: "immediately conduct or commission an independent investigation of the claims that some Falun Gong practitioners have been subjected to torture and used for organ transplants and take measures, as appropriate, to ensure that those responsible for such abuses are prosecuted and punished."

10) Lack of individual cases

The conclusion that Falun Gong have been killed in large numbers for their organs relies on the confluence of a number of evidentiary trails. This evidence does not necessarily identify individual victims. One response to the evidence that Falun Gong have been killed for their organs in the tens of thousands is, "name them".

This request to name individual cases may be made out of skepticism. Alternatively, the request to identify individual cases is made because activism around an individual case may be easier than advocacy around a general phenomenon. It is harder for the Government of China to skate round an inquiry when it is pointed, when we tell them the name of the victim, the date of the victimization and the place where it occurred.

To identify individual cases is inherently difficult for a number of reasons. One is that typically individual victimizations leave no traces behind.

In addition, the primary Falun Gong victims of organ harvesting are the non self-identified. Falun Gong refuse to identify themselves to their jailers to protect their friends, work places and families who are otherwise victimized for not having turned them in. Their jailers do not know who they are and their families do not know where they are. Those who victimize Falun Gong practitioners may know nothing about the practitioners other than that they are practitioners.

In principle, the need to identify individual victims should not matter. The evidence overall of the abuse is overwhelming even without identification of the individual victims.

Nonetheless, a few individual named cases have surfaced. Seven of these are mentioned in the book Bloody Harvest. An eighth was mentioned in a speech I delivered at a forum at the William Pitt Union, University of Pittsburgh, March 28, 2013[3].

Five of the eight cases mentioned in the book Bloody Harvest come from family members of victims. These family members of Falun Gong practitioners who died in detention reported seeing the corpses of their loved ones with surgical incisions and body parts missing. The authorities gave no coherent explanation for these mutilated corpses. There is no official explanation why the bodies were mutilated. Their mutilation is consistent with organ harvesting.

11) False symmetry

The Government of China slanders Falun Gong. Falun Gong practitioners condemn human rights violations inflicted by the Communist Party of China. To outsiders not paying much attention and unfamiliar with the Falun Gong, this dispute superficially looks like a foreign political slanging match. The tendency is not to get involved.

For media reporting a story where the dispute is relevant, there is a tendency to report what each side says, the Communist Party of China and Falun Gong practitioners, as they would do with any dispute, attempting to be neutral. The articles treat real violations inflicted by the Government of China and Chinese government propaganda about those violations on an equal footing.

The media, when referring to Falun Gong, will for instance sometimes say that followers describe Falun Gong in one way, while the Government of China considers it to be something else. The two assertions are juxtaposed without comment as if each should be treated equally seriously.

Research done on the killing of Falun Gong for their organs is treated similarly. The media, when they report the research, often juxtapose it with the most blatantly false and farfetched denials of the Communist Party/State, without any indication that the research is grounded in reality and that the foundation of the denials is easily observable fabrications.

The media will sometimes report that the research on the killing of Falun Gong for their organs is contested or controversial, without any indication that virtually the only contest or controversy comes from the Communist Party. There are, of course, some people who will repeat what the Communist party says without engaging in any serious research. The fact that all independent research has corroborated the initial research David Kilgour and I did about the killing of Falun Gong for their organs is put to one side. For some media, the differing quality of the evidence of either side has less interest than the fact of controversy.

Moreover, media, like the Communist Party, often attribute the research to a mythical Falun Gong organization or Falun Gong practitioners, with the implication that Falun Gong are an interested party. The fact that the research and evidence comes almost entirely from persons who are not Falun Gong practitioners is ignored.

Accusations of human rights violations are not always true and not always well intentioned. Those politically opposed to any regime will easily resort to false accusations of human rights violations as a means of delegitimizing that regime.

The difference between imagined human rights violations invented for purposes of delegitimization and actual human rights violations denied by the perpetrators is reality. We can not ignore reality and just consider charges and denials of human rights violations as a bunch of words all of equal weight.

The difference between Holocaust deniers and the tragic stories of the victims of the Holocaust is the real story, what actually happened. It would be irresponsible to feign neutrality between Holocaust deniers and Holocaust victims. Anyone concerned with truth, freedom and respect for human rights would disapprove strongly of those who treated Holocaust denial as a respectable opinion deserving the same weight and consideration as the tales of horror of Holocaust victims.

But Holocaust denial, like the Holocaust itself, is not an isolated experience. It is rather the most extreme form of a whole spectrum of speech abuses. Every grave human rights violation has its deniers. Perpetrators everywhere have a whole litany of sorry excuses; but the first line of defense for them all is "it did not happen".

The Communist Party of China has committed massive human rights violations against the Falun Gong. The Falun Gong are a group of innocents, a non-political non-violent community.

The Communist Party of China, to justify its brutal hold on power, does what communist parties have done everywhere— it admits nothing and denies everything. It manufactures phony charges, concocts facts, and imagines quotes. To put Chinese propaganda about the Falun Gong on the same level as evidence about the human rights violations perpetrated by the Communist Party of China, to create a false symmetry between them ignores reality and turns a blind eye to the monsters staring us in the face.

12) Indifference

Indifference is a general problem when we attempt to mobilize the public to oppose human rights violations. Though indifference is general, it is not uniform. Some human rights violations spark more of a public reaction than others.

The inactivity in response to the evidence on the killing of Falun Gong for their organs is particularly acute and explained by the accumulation of all other factors. The newness and seeming strangeness of Falun Gong, the wealth and weight of Communist China, the amount of evidence one needs to sort through to come to any firm conclusion, the Communist Party cover up, the newness of the violation, the onslaught of contrary Communist Party propaganda, the lack of structure of the Falun Gong community itself, the vestigial sympathy amongst left wing circles for Chinese communism, the improper shifting of the onus away from the Government of China, the absence of large numbers of identified individual cases, the false symmetry in which many reports engage between victims and perpetrators, have a cumulative, demobilizing effect.

When the natural inclination is to do nothing, when everyone is busy with their own lives and needs, there are just too many excuses this violation presents for disengagement. Caring begins with knowing. In this file, too many people do not care, because too many people do not know.

Though this is a difficult story to tell, for all the reasons listed, it is a story which must be told. Only by doing that can we hope to overcome the inattention from which this violation suffers.

---

[1] Jan Wong, "Feeling the long arm of China" Globe and Mail, August 6, 2005.

[2] See for instance http://www.facts.org.cn/Reports/World/201407/09/t20140709_1753443.htm

[3] "The Killing of Falun Gong for their Organs: Individual Cases"

http://endorganpillaging.org/2013/03/28/the-killing-of-falun-gong/

Jiang Zemin: The Ultimate Evil in the Destruction of Human Nature

By Theresa Chu

The CCP's organ harvesting death camps

In the morning of December 9, 2013, legal representatives and medical experts from six countries, including Canadian human rights lawyer David Matas, Executive Director of U.S. based Doctors Against Forced Organ Harvesting (DAFOH) Dr. Torsten Trey, Spanish human rights lawyer Carlos Jimenez Iglesias, British kidney specialist Dr. Adnan Sharif, French transplant surgeon Dr. Francis Navarro, and myself, a human rights lawyer from Taiwan, went to Geneva to meet with a UN lawyer and a China specialist representing the United Nations High Commissioner for Human Rights, Navi Pillay. We presented UN officials with discs of scanned DAFOH petitions calling for an end to the Chinese Communist Party's (CCP) forced organ harvesting of Falun Gong practitioners, which garnered approximately 1.5 million signatures. The signatures were collected from 53 countries and regions in five continents in five months.[1] Among the 1.5 million, the largest number—about 600,000—was from Asia. Nearly 5,000 physicians from Taiwan signed the petition appealing to the UN High Commissioner for Human Rights with the following requests:

1. Call upon China to immediately end forced organ harvesting of detained Falun Gong practitioners in China.

2. Initiate further investigations that lead to the prosecution of the perpetrators involved in this crime against humanity.

3. Call upon the Chinese government to immediately end the brutal persecution of Falun Gong, which is the root cause for forced organ harvesting of Falun Gong practitioners.

We expounded on the issue of China's organ harvesting program, sharing with them our investigations and professional analysis. We urged the UN to pay attention to the 1.5 million public appeals from all over the world. I also directly informed these officials that we have knowledge, from reliable sources, of the existence of death camps, or secret concentration camps where Falun Gong practitioners are detained and murdered through forced organ harvesting. Such death camps are in almost every city throughout China. I reminded the UN officials that it is their responsibility to investigate and locate these camps and stop the tragedy of this unprecedented human rights violation.

The officials did not question the source of the "death camp" allegations. They listened with somber attention, took notes, but did not respond. Faced with 1.5 million voices and the allegations of the existence of death camps, the officials' silence was disappointing, but not surprising. The UN's attitude in dealing with the Chinese Communist Party's human rights violations over the years had been taciturnity. Nonetheless, we have not given up our efforts to seek justice. In the West, it is said that, "To keep silence in the face of evil is to be cruel to good people."

In March and May of 2014, we visited the institutions of the European Union, the European Parliament, the U.S. State

Department, and the U.S. Congress, to further expose the ongoing atrocities of forced organ harvesting in China since the start of the persecution of Falun Gong. At every meeting, I explained, to the best of my knowledge, the death camps' existence in China and called for a swift investigation and an end to the CCP's crimes against humanity. Unfortunately, once again, officials did not ask for the source of these allegations, nor has there been any action to further investigate or to demand that the CCP immediately end its forced organ harvesting atrocities. While it is indeed difficult for the international community to deal with this issue, humankind must confront it with courage and must not sidestep this ongoing international human rights disaster.

During his tenure as the UN Special Rapporteur on Torture, Professor Manfred Nowak included the allegations of the CCP's organ harvesting from living Falun Gong practitioners in his 2007 and 2008 reports to the UN Human Rights Council. On November 8, 2011, in a public speech given at National Taiwan University, he made it abundantly clear that the investigative report on the CCP's organ harvesting of Falun Gong practitioners was "credible." [2] He said the evidence and data indicates that the source of organs in China has remained non-transparent, and that from the start of the persecution of Falun Gong, the number of organ transplants in China has dramatically surged. As the UN Special Rapporteur on Torture, Professor Nowak also sent a letter to specifically request that the Chinese government investigate the allegations on the issue of forced organ harvesting, make its organ transplant system transparent, and intensify penalties against the crime. However, the Chinese government has yet to respond. [3]

To date, the CCP is still unwilling to face up to the allegations of harvesting organs from living Falun Gong practitioners, and has turned a blind eye to the 2013 resolution passed by the European Parliament and the 2014 U.S. House of Representatives Foreign Affairs Committee resolution, both of which condemned the

CCP's organ harvesting of living Falun Gong practitioners, requested an international investigation and asked to bring the perpetrators to justice. During 2015, Chinese military doctors gradually came forward to testify against the military for colluding with the Chinese public security authorities and judicial bodies in the murderous acts of organ harvesting. Falun Gong Human Rights Attorney Group, DAFOH, Taiwan International Organ Transplant Care Association, and the World Organization to Investigate the Persecution of Falun Gong have collected incriminating evidence of CCP officials, judicial officers, and medical personnel, as well as urging international organizations to expose the government's dark secret of organ harvesting in an effort to stop these atrocities.

Meanwhile, people ask how the CCP could employ such brutal measures as live organ harvesting of Falun Gong practitioners and set up organ harvesting death camps against Falun Gong. If we probe deeper into the root cause, we will find that the key factor began in 1999, with then-CCP leader Jiang Zemin's aim to "eradicate Falun Gong," which became a guideline for the repression campaign. All of Jiang's accomplices were urged to use all means to implement the eradication. "Organ harvesting" and "death camps" were recklessly developed from such a destruction of human nature "extermination policy" led by Jiang.

The history of genocide shows that there must be an ambitious egomaniac with control over a nation, who—with pertinacious paranoia—will use all mechanisms to exterminate against any hated races or groups. The most tragic example of this was Hitler's atrocities against the Jewish people, while the most shocking extinction campaign in the 21st Century is Jiang's bloody suppression of over a hundred million Falun Gong practitioners in China.

In the early days when Jiang started his suppression of Falun

Gong and its adherents—numbering up to 100 million by the government's own estimates—he publicly declared that he would "eradicate Falun Gong in three months"[4] and ordered that this "strike-hard struggle" against Falun Gong must "ruin their reputation, bankrupt them financially, and eliminate them physically"[5]. Every Chinese person who was in any way associated with Falun Gong's tenets of "truthfulness, compassion, forbearance," regardless of sex, age or social class, were—and still continue to be—targets of the eradication campaign. This campaign was launched solely by Jiang. To reach this goal, he set up an "eradication mechanism" by using all party machines.

According to "The Convention on the Prevention and Punishment of the Crime of Genocide" adopted by the UN General Assembly on December 9, 1948, in the Resolution 260A (III), the crime of genocide in Article 2 is defined as "any of the following acts committed with intent to destroy, in whole or in part, a national, ethnical, racial or religious group, as such:

(a) Killing members of the group;

(b) Causing serious bodily or mental harm to members of the group;

(c) Deliberately inflicting on the group conditions of life calculated to bring about its physical destruction in whole or in part;

(d) Imposing measures intended to prevent births within the group;

(e) Forcibly transferring children of the group to another group."[6]

Jiang's open statement to exterminate Falun Gong and the subsequent nationwide "extinction implementation," led to tens of millions of innocent Falun Gong practitioners to be subjected to illegal arrests, brainwashing and torture to force them to give up their beliefs, murder, and even having their organs harvested. From Jiang's words and actions, it goes without saying that Jiang essentially admitted and confessed to the world that he was the culprit of the crime of genocide, the crimes against humanity, and the crime of torture in the persecution of Falun Gong.

Jiang Zemin is not only the violator of the three most serious crimes under international criminal laws, but he is also, above and beyond the ultimate evil in the destruction of humanity and human nature.

Jiang planned to eradicate Falun Gong within three months. His approach was to first manufacture "widespread hatred" toward Falun Gong among the general population, and then lead the entire nation onto a path of hatred for practitioners so as to promote the idea throughout the country that the "extermination campaign against Falun Gong is dealing with a public enemy." China has always had a strong tradition of respect and reverence toward gods and the heavens. The general public was not unfamiliar with Falun Dafa's spiritual beliefs. Among the 100 million who benefited from this cultivation practice, before the crackdown, were Party members and government officials who had openly given high praise to Falun Gong. Furthermore, the CCP had always been very clear that Falun Gong practitioners had neither ambition in politics nor interest in the affairs of the communist regime. Therefore, the only way Jiang could destroy the known goodness of Falun Gong was to take full advantage of all means and tactics of struggle that the CCP had accumulated since the beginning of its reign, by creating bigger lies and deeper hatred, as well as using more absolute violence to turn the original positive social ambience toward Falun Gong around.

What is also worth observing is that, although the Chinese people have repeatedly experienced the CCP's numerous political campaigns and are very well aware of the ruthlessness that the communist regime employs in eliminating political dissidents, most people have failed to realize that the essential prerequisite of Jiang's agenda to eradicate Falun Gong was to first "stir up people's instinct of being vicious and jettison humanity's most lofty nature of innate goodness."

Jiang's brutal tactics of banning the Chinese people from practicing and spreading Falun Gong, has not only infringed on Falun Gong practitioners' freedom of speech and expression, freedom of belief, and freedom of conscience, but has also completely obliterated the dissemination of Chinese culture and moral values. Poisoned by the Communist regime's lies and under CCP's threats and inducements, Chinese people have participated in the repression of good, innocent cultivators. It can reasonably be understood that once a person exercise his own conscience, it is very difficult for him or her to torture and harvest living organs from innocent cultivators. Only when the CCP reverses right and wrong, evil and goodness, and incites human's vicious nature, such atrocities as genocide can be carried out and maintained across the nation. Honestly speaking, to agitate Chinese people's hatred, misunderstanding, discrimination, and violence against a group of cultivators, Jiang aimed not only to eradicate Falun Gong, but also to destroy the Chinese people's most precious kindness and conscience.

Jiang establishes a pervasive extralegal eradication mechanism

As a head of state in 1999, Jiang set up a goal to exterminate Falun Gong within 3 months, He utilized all state and party machines to complete this goal. But "eradication" is not legally allowed in the West or the East. Bypassing constitutional law and other domestic laws, he established an extrajudicial mechanism to execute his genocide plan, penetrating from the Central government down to all local jurisdictions. On June 10, 1999—about a month before the nationwide suppression of Falun Gong—Jiang personally set up a specialized mechanism solely dedicated to persecuting Falun Gong, similar to the Nazis' Gestapo and the Communist Cultural Revolution Group: The "CCP Central Committee Leadership Team to Handle the Falun Gong Issue," its executive office is known as the "610 Office", a reference to its date of origin. According to the report of the World Organization to Investigate the Persecution of Falun Gong, the set up or operations of the Leadership Team and its 610 Office are classified information, which the CCP has never made public.[7]

Although Jiang was unable to bring about the eradication of Falun Gong within his timeline, he was effective in establishing a full mechanism of genocide whose tentacles have stretched to the local districts and have taken root throughout the country. There is no public record of when all the various levels of leadership teams, from the CCP's Central government to every province, city, county, district, and township, were established. After the crackdown commenced, all 610 Offices without any legal authorization, began to direct and coordinate the nation's administrative and judicial mechanism, including the departments of public security, procuratorate, administration of justice, security and others, to investigate, arrest, prosecute, and bring to trial all participants of Falun Gong activities. According to incomplete statistics, there are at least one million full-time and part-time staff working at different levels in a multitude of 610 Offices throughout China, enjoying ample funding, subject only to the Party Committee and to the highest level of the 610 Office.

Since the Cultural Revolution, Jiang has been the only CCP leader to capitalize on his position, maximizing all government resources in a highly organized, coordinated effort—extrajudicial mechanism—to persecute the Chinese people. Since the start of the persecution since 1999, the 610 Party machine has been running day and night, from the urban districts to rural regions, severely torturing Falun Gong practitioners physically, in an extreme effort to transform their spiritual beliefs.

Jiang not only used the Leadership Team and the 610 Office to persecute Falun Gong practitioners in mainland China, but also extended the 610 Office's persecutory function overseas. Under the direction of the 610 Office, Chinese embassies and consulates throughout the world have collected information on and disrupted Falun Gong activities overseas. In 2005, former First Secretary of the Chinese General Consulate in Sydney Australia, Chen Yonglin, revealed in an interview with ABC Australian Television that the 610 System not only exists, but senior officials of the Central 610 Office had also visited Sydney to check on his job performance and demand that he strengthen his efforts in the persecution of Falun Gong.[8] The same year, Hao Fengjun, former official of the 610 Office in Tianjin, who sought political asylum from the Australian government, disclosed in a media interview during a visit to Taiwan, an inside story that the CCP Central Committee had issued documents framing Falun Gong.[9]

Jiang, with envy and hatred toward Falun Gong, concocted an atmosphere of terror in Chinese society with his hand-picked and personally nurtured posse members that included former director of the Political and Legal Affairs Committee (PLAC), Luo Gan, Chinese security Tsar, Zhou Yongkang, the infamous Bo Xilai, Xu Caihou, and others, turning "the entire Chinese society into a big prison," treating kind and gentle Falun Gong practitioners as enemies, breaking up many families of Falun Gong practitioners. On the evening of February 8, 2002, Yang Lirong, a 34-year-old female Falun Gong practitioner of North Gate Street, Dingzhou City, Baoding district, Hebei Province, was strangled to death by her husband. The husband, a driver for the Bureau of Standard

Measurement, could not withstand the unrelenting pressure of harassment and intimidation by the police. Terrified of losing his job, he grabbed his wife's throat the morning after a police visit, causing her death by suffocation, rendering their ten-year-old son without a mother. He immediately reported the incident to the police, who arrived at the scene within minutes. They promptly cut his wife open and removed her organs from her still warm body. An official from the Dingzhou Public Security Bureau exclaimed, "That was not an autopsy! That was operating on a living person!" [Minghui.org September 22, 2004 report].

In Wanjia Forced Labor Camp in Heilongjiang Province, a female practitioner about six to seven months pregnant, was placed on a stool with her wrists tied up with heavy ropes on a beam ten feet from the floor. One end of the rope was attached to a pulley on the beam, the other end was held in the hands of a prison guard. The stool was kicked away from under her so that she was left hanging. The guard would periodically ease up on the rope, and she would rapidly fall down. When the guard pulled on the rope, she would be hung up again. The pregnant woman was thus tortured this way in succession until an involuntary miscarriage was induced. The cruelty of this act was compounded by the fact that her husband was forced to be present to witness his wife being tortured.[10]

Under Jiang Zemin's mad wish to eradicate Falun Gong in both flesh and spirit, the victimized have not only been Falun Gong practitioners but also their families and friends. Lawyers that have come forward to defend Falun Gong practitioners ended up being persecuted and tortured as well. These lawyers include Gao Zhisheng, who became widely known as "the conscience of China," Tang Jitian, Wang Yonghang, and other lawyers. In addition, there are numerous citizens who were implicated in the persecution for signing petitions officially with their fingerprints in red ink to request the court to release innocent Falun Gong practitioners in their neighborhoods. A conservative estimate indicates that, on top of the 100 million Falun Gong practitioners who are suffering under Jiang Zemin's persecution since 1999, there are several times that number of Chinese people who are enduring physical and mental suffering from the CCP's persecution of Falun Gong.

Even worse, the CCP officials who have been swept up into participating in the persecution, frightened that they would be brought to justice after Jiang stepped down, are trying their best to induce more people into joining the persecution, forming alliances of accomplices so that they all will have blood on their hands, and in the shroud of silence no one will be held accountable and the suppression can continue unabated. Jiang himself, after stepping down from power—fearful of being held accountable for his evil deeds, went to extremes to ascertain that his original posse in the military and in the Politburo, including Zhou Yongkang, the Secretary of the Central Political Bureau Standing Committee as well as the PLAC in command of all public security, and others in the CCP's Central major systems, would continue to maintain the brutal persecution of Falun Gong.

Jiang's persecution of Falun Gong can indeed be called "the biggest human rights disaster of the 21st century"

1. **Extent of the persecution:** In addition to the Chinese mainland, the persecution has extended to Taiwan, Hong Kong, and other countries and regions where there are Falun Gong practitioners and CCP Consulates.

2. **Mechanisms and means of the persecution:** The mechanisms involve the comprehensive use of all diplomatic, military, national security, education, propaganda, administrative, judicial and financial systems. The means include

brainwashing, prolonged violent beatings, baton shocks, gang rape and sexual assault, administration of psychotropic drugs, forced labor, sleep deprivation, slandering, forcing practitioners to give up their beliefs and admit guilt, coercing other practitioners to recant, sham trial, denial of justice, vicious forced-feeding, and so on.

The most notorious is the Masanjia Labor Camp, where Falun Gong practitioners are subjected to as many as 20 different kinds of torture methods.[11] Yi Liping, a female Falun Gong practitioner from Tieling City, Liaoning Province, was sent to Masanjia Labor Camp three times for a total of 18 months. In April 19, 2001, she and eight other female Falun Gong practitioners were put into male prison cells at the Zhang Shi Male Labor Camp in Liaoning Province. Several were tortured to death, some suffered from mental disorders while in detention, and others choose to remain silent under high pressure. Beijing resident Liu Hua was sent to Masanjia Labor Camp for appealing to the government. Liu recalled, "My cellmate Xin Shuhua, from Benxi city, Liaoning Province, told me that she was one of the 18 female Falun Gong practitioners who was locked up in a male prison cell where they were all gang raped repeatedly."[12]

Overseas, the CCP uses its embassies and consulates not only to collect personal information of Falun Gong practitioners and their relatives and friends, but also to conspire with pro-CCP media to slander Falun Gong overseas, paying gangsters to attack Falun Gong and disrupt Falun Gong anti-persecution activities. Particularly in the United States, Canada, South America, Australia, Taiwan, and Hong Kong, the pro-CCP thugs to harass and assault Falun Gong practitioners who clarify the truth and expose the atrocities of the persecution to Chinese and other tourists in major tourist attractions. Their tactics include incitement to hatred, violence, and damage to property.

Of all the CCP's forms of persecution, the most heinous one has to be forced organ harvesting from Falun Gong practitioners. In 2006 in Washington, DC, when a nurse with the alias of Annie, whose ex-husband was a neurosurgeon at the Liaoning Provincial Thrombosis Hospital, and a Chinese reporter with the alias of Peter came forward to share their knowledge of the CCP's crimes. After their reports, Canadian human rights lawyer David Matas and former Canadian MP for the Asia Pacific region David Kilgour conducted an independent investigation into the allegations of China's organ harvesting practices. With 52 pieces of evidence, they confirmed that the allegations of live organ harvesting were true, and called the CCP's crime "an unprecedented evil on this planet."[13]

3. **Number of persecuted victims:** Jiang started persecuting Falun Gong on July 20, 1999, depriving 100 million Falun Gong practitioners in China their fundamental rights, freedom of speech, belief, and assembly. Over the past 16 years, it has been difficult to estimate how many Falun Gong practitioners have been tortured, murdered, or killed for their organs. Countless overseas Falun Gong practitioners were attacked by thugs. Also, countless family members of Falun Gong practitioners have also suffered from the persecution.

4. **Expenses of the persecution:** At a 2003 press conference at the Canadian Parliament "Jiang Zemin's Regime Draws Upon Massive National Financial Resources In Its Persecution of Falun Gong," the World Organization to Investigate the Persecution of Falun Gong, by invitation of the Canadian Members of Parliament, presented a list of findings, which included a 4.2 billion yuan investment to construct brainwashing centers in December 2001. On July 4,

2001, ABC reported that almost half of the detainees in labor camps were Falun Gong practitioners.

In order to hold increasing numbers of Falun Gong prisoners, many provinces and cities spent large amount of money to build or expand labor camps. The Shanxi Province labor camp relocation project's total investment amounted to 19.37 million yuan.

In order to stimulate and encourage more perpetrators to participate in the persecution of Falun Gong, the Masanjia Labor Camp Director Su and Deputy Director Shao were rewarded 50 thousand yuan and 30 thousand yuan, respectively. In many areas, the reward for capturing a Falun Gong practitioner has reached several thousand yuan or even more than 10 thousand yuan. In 2001, inside information from the CCP's Ministry of Public Security revealed that the cost of arresting Falun Gong practitioners in Tiananmen Square alone was between 1.7 million and 2.5 million yuan per day, or from 620 million to 910 million yuan per year.

From cities to remote rural areas, the local police force, the security bureaus, and officials from the 610 Office, hunt down Falun Gong practitioners everywhere. Reports estimate that Jiang hired at least a few million people to do his dirty work. Their total wages, bonuses, overtime pay, and subsidies for persecuting innocent people accounted for hundreds of billions of yuan each year.

According the report by Taiwan Central News Agency in March 2003, on February 27, 2001, Jiang Zemin appropriated 4 billion yuan to install surveillance cameras aimed at monitoring Falun Gong practitioners. Large numbers of slanderous propaganda materials were published in various formats including books, brochures, VCDs and posters. At least two movies and a 20-episode anti-Falun Gong TV series were made to defame Falun Gong. A quarter of China's economic resources are used to persecute Falun Gong, and it is one of reasons that the persecution can continue.

The source of funds are misappropriated from investments, common citizens' hard-earned money, along with hefty illegal fines imposed on Falun Gong practitioners, their families, and their work units. Vast sums of money are spent on public security, national security, 610 Offices, and foreign affairs for persecution purpose.[14]

5. **Continuity of the persecution:** Starting from July 20, 1999, the day Jiang Zemin officially announced the suppression of Falun Gong, to date, every day, without interruption.

Despite the unprecedented viciousness of this human rights disaster, Jiang's intention to "eliminate Falun Gong" has been doomed to fail from the beginning. Although the CCP's repression tactics to "destroy," "struggle," and "strike hard" have been effective in the past, for Falun Dafa practitioners, with their staunch adherence to the tenets of "truthfulness, compassion, forbearance," no amount of physical or sexual assault, no amount of electric shocks and no amount of extreme torture can deprive them of their spiritual beliefs. There are innumerable cases of Falun Gong practitioners who had been forced and coerced by the CCP to write "confessions" and "guarantees," later return to their beliefs.[15]

Largest international human rights lawsuit of the 21st century

The collaboration of Jiang and the CCP in the persecution of Falun Gong has resulted in the denial of justice for Falun Gong practitioners and in the persecution of their defense lawyers in China. On August 25, 2000, the second year of the repression, two Falun Gong practitioners filed criminal complaints with the Chinese Supreme People's Procuratorate and the Chinese Supreme People's Court against Jiang Zemin, Zeng Qinghong (Secretary of the Secretariat of the CCP Central Committee), and Luo Gan (Secretary of the Political and Legal Affairs Committee), for persecuting Falun Gong. They were immediately and secretly arrested by the police. One died, the other was injured.[16]

After multiple failures to urge Jiang to end the persecution, overseas Falun Gong practitioners have filed criminal complaints, launched private prosecutions, and civil lawsuits against Jiang and his cohorts in 30 countries all over the world since 2002. Falun Gong Human Rights Attorney Group refers to those lawsuits against Jiang and other perpetrators as the "Global Lawsuit Against Jiang." Falun Gong practitioners have filed criminal complaints and civil lawsuits against Jiang and other perpetrators in national courts overseas for their genocide, torture, and crimes against humanity, most serious crime under international criminal laws. In those legal proceedings, Falun Gong practitioners asked the courts to exercise universal jurisdiction and to issue a warrant to arrest defendants Jiang and other perpetrators. The "Global Lawsuit Against Jiang" is—in a most noble and upright manner— to clarify the truth of the persecution and to seek justice in democratic countries, after Falun Gong practitioners' efforts failed in China's judicial system and in the International Criminal Court.

Considering the number of national courts Falun Gong practitioners filed criminal complaints and civil lawsuits with, the ranks of the CCP leadership and senior officials being sued, and the transnational scale of human rights lawyers, "Global Lawsuit Against Jiang" can be called "the largest international human rights lawsuits of the 21st century." It is unprecedented. In the "Global Lawsuit Against Jiang", Jiang Zemin, Luo Gan, Liu Jing, Zhou Yongkang, Zeng Qinghong, and Bo Xilai, are considered the most notorious Party officials seriously involved in the persecution of Falun Gong. Hong Kong's and Taiwan's Falun Gong practitioners persecuted in mainland China have also launched a private prosecution and a civil lawsuit in Taiwan and Hong Kong courts, respectively against Jiang, Li Lanqing, and Luo Gan for genocide and torture.

On November 2009, the Spanish National Court prosecuted against Jiang, Luo Gan, Bo Xilai, Jia Qinglin and Wu Guanzheng for their persecution of Falun Gong, charging them with the crimes of genocide and torture. The following month, the Argentine federal court issued an international warrant to arrest Jiang and Luo Gan for their persecution of Falun Gong, charging them with crimes against humanity. At the time, the Hong Kong and Taiwan media, The Washington Post, The New York Times, and Voice of America, and other international media all reported the incident. A Chinese Foreign Ministry spokesman came forward with a threat, claiming the arrest warrant affected the relations between China and Argentina. [17] Jiang became the first former country leader and CCP party head to have been issued arrest warrants by a foreign court.

According to incomplete statistics of the Falun Gong Human Rights Attorney Group [18], the general situation of "Global Lawsuit Against Jiang" is summarized below:

1. Countries or territories where Falun Gong practitioners filed criminal complaints, private prosecution or civil lawsuits against former Chinese leader Jiang Zemin for genocide, crimes against humanity and torture:
  • Europe: Belgium, Spain, Germany, Greece, the Netherlands, Sweden
  • America: United States, Canada, Bolivia, Chile, Argentina, Peru
  • Asia: Taiwan, Hong Kong, Japan, South Korea

- Oceania: Australia, New Zealand

2.   Countries and territories where Falun Gong practitioners filed criminal complaints or civil action against CCP officials for genocide, crimes against humanity and torture:
  - Europe: France, Germany, Belgium, Holland, Sweden, Finland, Armenia, Moldova, Iceland, Spain, Sweden, Ireland, Denmark, Cypress, Russia, Austria, Switzerland
  - Americas: United States, Canada, Bolivia, Chile, Argentina, Peru
  - Asia: Taiwan, Hong Kong, Japan, Korea
  - Oceana: Australia, New Zealand
  - Africa: Tanzania

3. The incumbent or former CCP officials in the aforementioned countries or territories against whom Falun Gong practitioners filed criminal complaints or civil lawsuits:
  - Luo Gan (Political and Legal Affairs Committee Secretary)
  - Zhou Yongkang (Minister of Public Security, Political and Legal Affairs Committee Secretary)
  - Zeng Qinghong (Vice Chairman)
  - Bo Xilai (Minister of Commerce)
  - Li Lanqing (State Council Vice Premier)
  - Liu Jing (Deputy Minister of Public Security)
  - Zhao Zhifei (Hubei Province Public Security Bureau Chief)
  - Liu Qi (Beijing mayor)
  - Li Changchu (CCP Politburo Standing Committee Member)
  - Xia Deren (Liaoning Provincial Party Committee Deputy Secretary)
  - Wu Guanzheng (Shandong Provincial Party Committee Secretary)
  - Wang Maolin (Central 610 Office Manager)
  - Wang Xudong (Minister of Chinese Ministry of

Information Industry, Hebei Provincial Party Committee Secretary)

- Zhao Zhizhen (Wuhan City Radio and Television Bureau Chief)
- Chen Zhili (Minister of Education)
- Jia Qinglin (Beijing Municipal Committee Secretary, Chinese People's Political Consultative Committee Chairman)
- Su Rong (Gansu Provincial Party Committee Secretary)
- Xu Guangchun (Henan Province CCP Party Committee Secretary)
- Huang Huahua (Guangdong Province Governor)
- Wang Sanyun (Anhui Province Governor)
- Ji Lin (Beijing City Vice Mayor)
- Zhao Zhengyong (Shaanxi Province Acting Governor)
- Chen Zhenggao (Liaoning Province Governor)
- Wang Zuoan (State Bureau of Religious Affairs Bureau Chief)
- Ye Xiaowen (State Bureau of Religious Affairs Bureau Chief)
- Yang Song (Hubei Province Party Committee Deputy Secretary, local head of 610 Office)
- Huang Ju (State Council Vice Premier)
- Guo Chuanjie (Chinese Academy of Sciences Deputy Secretary, 610 Office Vice Group Leader)
- Li Yuanwei (Liaoning Province Lingyuan Prison Management Bureau Chief, local head of 610 Office)
- Jia Chunwang (Public Security Former Minister)
- Lin Yanchi (Jilin Province Provincial Committee Deputy Secretary, 610 Office Group Leader)
- Sun Jiazheng (Chinese People's Political Consultative Committee Vice Chairman, Ministery of Culture Former Minister)
- Wang Yusheng (China Anti-Cult Association Vice Chairman)

- Wang Taihua (Anhui Province Provincial Party Committee Secretary)
- Zhang Dejiang (Guangdong Province Provincial Committee Secretary)
- Chen Shaoji (Guangdong Province Political and Legal Affairs Committee Secretary)
- Shi Honghui (Guangdong Province Bureau Chief of Reeducation Through Labor Secretary and Party Committee Secretary)
- Guo Jinlong (Beijing City Mayor)
- Qiang Wei (Jiangxi Province Provincial Party Committee Secretary)

4. Chinese embassies and overseas Communist organizations which Falun Gong practitioners have filed criminal complaints against, and civil lawsuits for battery and assault, destruction of property, harassment, slander and libel: USA, Indonesia, Canada, Germany, Korea, Russia, Malaysia, Japan, and the Philippines. In addition, Pan Xinchun, Canadian Chinese Embassy Deputy Counsel General; Li Bin, Korean Chinese Embassy Ambassador; Zhang Xin, Korean Chinese Embassy Counselor and five other counselors; also Sun Xiangyang, Malaysia Chinese Embassy Information Officer; and others have been charged.

5. Falun Gong practitioners also filed legal complaints with International Criminal Court, the UN Committee against Torture, the UN Commission on Human Rights (formerly UN Human Rights Council), the European Court of Human Rights against Jiang, Zeng Qinghong, and the 610 Office for their persecution against Falun Gong.

Conclusion: "Beijing Trial" is a historical requirement

The wicked perpetrators of heinous crimes must face historic evaluation and should be tried in the court. Humanity as a whole, regardless of race or creed, craves justice and believes that good and evil will both be reciprocated in kind. Wisdom is gained and lessons are learned from past experiences. What can be understood from history can serve as a most vital tool in our search for peace and prosperity for humankind.

After World War II, the "Nuremberg Trial" prompted human society to develop mechanisms to punish international heinous crimes, significantly impacting the advancement of international human rights laws. After the Trial, the International Human Rights Convention was developed for the prevention and punishment of crimes of genocide, crimes against humanity, torture and other international norms to hold individuals accountable. The International Criminal Court came into being after that. The development of all these international justice mechanisms proves that atrocities must not be tolerated by mankind. Praising good and punishing evil will always be the standard for human history.

Jiang and countless numbers of officials at all levels in the Chinese government have played a role in planning and implementing the vicious persecution of Falun Gong. There is no better way to close this tragic page of history than to bring Communist villains who are responsible for the persecution of Falun Gong to trial.

Jiang Zemin and his posse should be brought to justice in China, so that the Chinese people for all generations to come will forever remember these lessons in history, so that such heinous crimes so devoid of humanity will never happen again. The persecution of Falun Gong is a test of human conscience. After decades of torture, brutal repression and mass murder, the disintegration of the CCP is inevitable. A "Beijing Trial" is a necessary requirement. It is imperative!

[1] Theresa Chu: Calling on the UN to investigate the CCP's "live organ harvesting concentration camps." http://www.epochtimes.com/b5/14/7/23/n4207441.htm

[2] Former UN High Commissioner: Allegations of CCP's organ harvesting is credible.
http://big5.minghui.org/mh/articles/2011/11/11/%E5%89%8D%E%81%AF%E5%90%88%E5%9C%8B%E5%B0%88%E5%93%A1-%E5%B0%8D%E4%B8%AD%E5%85%B1%E6%B4%BB%E6%91%98%E5%99%A8%E5%AE%98%E6%8C%87%E6%8E%A7%E5%8F%AF%E4%BF%A1%EF%B-C%88%E5%9C%96%EF%BC%89%-249086.htm

CCP live organ harvesting of Falun Gong practitioners report (5).
http://big5.minghui.org/mh/articles/2012/11/7/%E4%B8%AD%E5%85%B1%E6%B4%BB%E9%AB%94%E6%91%98%E5%8F%96%E6%B3%95%E8%BC%AA%E5%8A%9F%E5%AD%B8%E5%93%A1%E5%99%A8%E5%AE%98%E5%A0%B1%E5%91%8A%EF%B-C%88%E4%BA%94%EF%BC%89-265162.html

[3] CCP live organ harvesting of Falun Gong practitioners report (1)
http://www.xinsheng.net/xs/articles/big5/2012/11/19/49074p.html

[4] Jiang Zemin's distorted sense of envy toward Falun Gong's founder, Master Li Hongzhi.
http://www.epochweekly.com/b5/394/14023p5.htm

Photos of CCP's war on Falun Gong from failed eradication attempts to protracted struggles to final war in recent years.
http://tw.aboluowang.com/2014/0813/429444.html#sthash.xO2JE2IQ.dpbs

[5] Infighting exacerbated due to blood debt. http://www.epochweekly.com/b5/257/10244.htm

[6] Detailed content of UN Convention.
http://www.un.org/chinese/hr/issue/docs/85.PDF

[7] World Organization to Investigate the Persecution of Falun Gong (WOIP-FG) Report (IX): Report on the "610 Office" – Central.
http://www.epochtimes.com/b5/4/10/26/n700451.htm

"History Today"; Gestapo-style CCP's 610 Office name change
http://www.epochtimes.com/b5/14/10/14/n4271937.htm

[8] Chen Yonglin: Central 610 officials went to the Consulate to inspect job performance.
http://www.epochtimes.com/b5/5/6/21/n960607.htm

[9] Taiwan's Central Broadcasting Radio Station interviewed Hao Fengjun.
http://www.epochtimes.com/b5/5/12/27/n1168126.htm

Former 610 Official Hao Fengjun testified that the CCP persecutes Falun Gong with false accusations.
http://big5.minghui.org/mh/articles/2005/6/12/103923.htm

[10] Nine Commentaries on the Communist Party Commentary Five: On the Collusion of Jiang Zemin and the Chinese Communist Party to Persecute Falun Gong.
http://www.epochtimes.com/b5/4/11/27/n730058.htm

[11] Partial list of extreme tortures conducted at the Masanjia Forced Labor Camp.
http://huiyuan.minghui.org/big5/html/articles/2006/3/6302.html

[12] Du Bin's new book published in Hong Kong exposes again sexual torture at Masanjia.
http://www.epochtimes.com/b5/14/7/23/n4207573.htm

[13] For details please refer to and Bloody Harvest published by the Broad Press
http://www.books.com.tw/products/0010508143

[14] Central News Agency (CAN): The CCP government spent large amount of national financial resources to persecute Falun Gong.
http://big5.minghui.org/mh/articles/2003/3/23/46962.html
http://www.zhuichaguoji.org/sites/default/files/record/2004/05/132-ji-ang_ze_min_ji_tuan_2.pdf

[15] Minghui.org website's collection of solemn declarations to resume Falun Gong practice by practitioners who had been coerced to renounce Falun Dafa or to write repentance statements.
http://big5.minghui.org/mh/fenlei/85/

[16] Multimillionaire brings lawsuit against the leading culprit of Falun Gong persecution.
http://weekend.minghui.org/big5/343/343_05.HTM

[17] Accountability liquidation about to commence, Jiang Zemin becomes the first General Secretary to receive arrest warrants issued by foreign countries.
http://www.epochtimes.com/b5/14/2/11/n4080335.htm

[18] "Falun Gong Human Rights Attorney Group" is made up of overseas Falun Gong lawyer practitioners and other qualified lawyers who have been appointed by Falun Gong practitioners worldwide to bring lawsuits against Jiang Zemin, the leading culprit of the Falun Gong persecution. The list in the "global lawsuit against Jiang" mentioned herein is aggregated from information provided by members of this global group of lawyers.

An Extreme Evil on Earth

Becoming Aware of China's Genocide and Taking Action

By Carlos Iglesias Jimenez

When we analyze the concept of genocide described in the *Convention on the Prevention and Punishment of the Crime of Genocide* from December 9th, 1948, we realize how far human evilness can reach. If there are leaders of certain dictatorships who are capable of exterminating groups of people for ethnic, racial or religious reasons, then this means that the degeneration of human values has reached its maximum level.

Throughout history, genocides took place with the participation or complicity of the highest circles of power under dictatorial regimes. Any and all means available within a state's disposal, including economic and strategic resources, would be utilized to accomplish the goal of eliminating an entire group of innocent human beings.

Using a wide range of methods, from domestic as well as international propaganda campaigns to murder, the persecution of Falun Gong initiated under the former head of the Chinese Communist Party (CCP), Jiang Zemin, in 1999 and carried out by all levels of the government, aims to completely eradicate the adherents of this belief system. Brainwashing, aimed at forcing Falun Gong practitioners to give up their beliefs and "transform" their thinking to better reflect Party ideology, torture—which is often so abusive that it leads to death and forced organ harvesting, which always results in a Falun Gong practitioner's demise; actions that fulfill the definition of the crime of genocide as stated in Articles II and III of the 1948 Convention. In recent history, the Rwandan genocide claimed at least 500,000 deaths in 1994 and the Srebrenica genocide claimed more than 8,000 deaths in 1995. Since 1999, more than 100 million practitioners of Falun Gong have been subject to brutal, state-run persecution in China and worldwide.

It is usually, if not always the case, that genocide is denounced only after it has developed from its early stages, when countless lives have been tragically lost. This is most certainly the case for the innocent victims in China who practice Falun Gong (otherwise known as Falun Dafa), a peaceful and spiritual self-improvement system based on the principles of truthfulness, compassion and tolerance.

When the *Convention* on genocide was adopted by the United Nations in 1948, it seemed that a collective conscience had emerged; that a higher evolution of humanitarian values aimed to protect lives, human dignity and peoples' beliefs.

But what remained unnoticed is that in those very moments after World War II, what was taking shape in the East, and more specifically in China, was the most destructive, cruel and heartless dictatorship of human history. The CCP, a tyrannical regime that not only tries to destroy a large segment of its own people— millions of well-meaning people, who are trying to improve their morality and compassion for all beings—but is benefiting from their destruction, killing tens of thousands on demand for their organs.

This is the reality that was made clear to me by many victims of these terrible crimes. And in hearing about these horrendous tragedies, I felt compelled to act within my power as an attorney to help these innocent people. I was fortunate to be able to draw upon the Spanish Laws of universal jurisdiction established in the Organic Law of Judicial Power of Spain. Article 23 of the Laws was, at the time, the most advanced law in the world with regard to the protection of global justice, as it allowed for the possibility of persecuting perpetrators of genocide or torture regardless of their nationality and of the nationality of their victims.

My personal journey to combat the genocide of Falun Dafa practitioners

My interviews with the victims were quite intense; their stories recalled such immense suffering, it was difficult for me to bear the anguish I experienced in listening to them. However, I was touched by their steadfast faith and will to obtain justice. Their greatest wish was for people around the world to no longer be deceived by the CCP's propaganda but instead to be fully aware of the brutality of the persecution.

The decision to take action could not be delayed, as there were a series of circumstances at that time that seemed to make the CCP invulnerable to prosecution for genocide.

These circumstances included:

1. The impossibility of bringing criminals in China to justice (what is known as *territorial principle*) because the CCP is precisely who has the power and exercises control of the genocide in China.

2. The CCP has not signed the Rome Statute that established the International Criminal Court (ICC), making it impossible to take these crimes before the ICC, because its jurisdiction is not recognized.

3. The CCP has the right of veto in the United Nations

Security Council, making it impossible for the United Nations to take specific actions against China. This protective wall of the Chinese Communist Party could and should only be demolished with a universal jurisdiction, based on the laws of countries like Spain, and at the same time could serve as a loudspeaker to let the world know the truth of these terrible crimes against humanity

The only thing left for me was to go with my heart and act.

Thanks to the help and collaboration of my colleague Dr. Terri Marsh, Executive Director and Senior Litigation partner of the Human Rights Law Foundation, as well as the interviews with several Falun Dafa practitioners and relatives of practitioners killed or tortured in China, I filed a lawsuit in Spain on October 15, 2003 against the primary party responsible for this atrocity, Jiang Zemin, for the crimes of genocide and torture.

Under Jiang's rule as leader of the CCP, three actions and specific instructions on Falun Gong practitioners were ordered: "Defame their reputations, ruin them financially and destroy them physically." Together with Jiang, the lawsuit also named Luo Gan, the coordinator and executor of the 610 Office, which controlled the persecution against Falun Dafa. I call it the "Chinese Gestapo," whose mission was not different than operating for the state, above the law and without any control, in order to identify and illegally detain Falun Dafa practitioners. The *610 Office* also instructs forced labor camps, where practitioners are tortured to death.

One important aspect of this tragedy is that all the logistics of the persecution and the propaganda by the CCP apparatus requires huge amounts of the national budget, financed by Chinese citizens and used for the sole purpose of eliminating a significant part of its own people. What kind of leadership eradicates its own people? Is the CCP worthy of representing a nation with a history of 5,000 years, carrying the suffering of its own innocent citizens with their blood on its flag?

The intense statewide propaganda has served to generate the government's hatred of Falun Dafa while intending to turn the Chinese people away from what had been a hugely popular and widely embraced practice. Before the crackdown on July 20, 1999, up to 100 million Chinese people—by the government's estimates—were improving their minds and bodies through this peaceful cultivation system. Initially, the media boasted of the practice's benefits to society—the government was saving billions on health care—but this took a dramatic turn as the government applied in full force its agenda of elimination. The strategy of genocide began with countless lies, defamations and slander. The CCP utilized the strength of the entire media—mainly state-run television, radio, press and news agencies—to build a huge mountain of fabricated lies about Falun Dafa.

The aim was to disarm the conscience of the Chinese people, to render the nation insensitive to the ban on Falun Dafa. This way, a clear message was sent to the Chinese people, warning the population how dangerous it is to have beliefs that are not in line with those of the CCP.

The arbitrary and illegal detentions were on the rise every day, according to the Human Rights Commission of the United Nations and NGOs such as Amnesty International and Human Rights Watch. Reports of thousands of Falun Dafa practitioners were locked up in prisons and forced labor camps without judicial guarantees, where, under the most wrenching horror, the most unimaginable form of torture that a human being had ever known was taking place.

Until now, I had been unable to communicate in writing or share in public discourse the terrible pain that so many thousands of innocent people were suffering in the darkness of forced labor camps in China. I felt such tremendous despair before the testimonies of the victims. I could only mourn when Dai Zhizhen, with her daughter Fadu in her arms, told me the story of her husband's cruel murder; I could only mourn when I personally heard the story of painter Zhang Cui Ying, who suffered terrible torture of mind and body for practicing Falun Dafa; I could only mourn when then-student Zhao Ming thoroughly described how he was forced to squat daily for over ten hours a day with his heels raised, how he received electric shocks on his body and was forbidden to sleep, that he was handcuffed to a chair and beaten by guards every time he closed his eyes; or how Falun Dafa practitioner Chen Yin suffered the greatest humiliation that a woman can endure, forcibly undressed and thrown into a cell with male prisoners, where she was sexually assaulted, and then drenched with ice cold water for days on end.

The original lawsuit against Jiang and Luo Gan was followed by additional lawsuits in Spain against senior leaders of the CCP who were directly involved in the persecution of Falun Dafa, specifically Jia Qinglin, Wu Wangzhen and then-Minister of Commerce Bo Xilai. Bo had previously held the posts of governor of Liaoning Province and mayor of Dalian City, and was directly responsible for the largest massacre against Falun Dafa practitioners in the province's labor camps as well as being one of the principle perpetrators of live organ harvesting of Falun Dafa practitioners.

All of the lawsuits followed the process of universal justice in Spain and numerous investigations were conducted, bringing to light evidence that demonstrated the horrors and tragedies of the evil deeds committed by the CCP against its own people.

The most terrible atrocity, however, was yet to come to my knowledge, something unconscionable to any human being, something that made me shudder and left me deeply shaken, the greatest crime in the history of mankind: the harvesting and sale of organs from living people. At first I was unable to believe it, as no one belonging to the human race could reach this extent of wickedness and evil, but this was a reality: Under a state-sanctioned program, organs were being harvested from thousands of live, healthy Falun Dafa practitioners, so that the government could reap financial gain.

The questions I asked myself were no longer that of a lawyer, but of a human being:

What kind of demon is the CCP, which actively promotes, coordinates and reaps benefits from the mass, forced removal of organs from their own people?

What kind of evil entity is one that, once the organs are forcibly harvested, incinerates the corpses in order to dispose of the evidence, only to charge large sums of money for each organ harvested, upwards of $150,000 for a liver or a pair of kidneys?

What sort of criminal minds, absolutely diabolical, are capable of creating and developing a corrupt organization, whose multi-million dollar revenues come from killing thousands of people and who have turned this atrocity into a lifestyle?

How can they lead the Chinese nation and represent the Chinese people, who they torture, murder and allow their bodies to be carved into pieces and sold?

I finally understood the extent of the tragedy, the enormous horror that is the CCP, which sells to the Western world an image of a prosperous economy and soaring middle class, and yet hides the fact that much of their products are made under torture in labor camps—at no cost—by an army of hundreds of thousands of innocent people; prisoners of conscience who, under torture, are forced to work continuously for 16 or 18 hours a day, in order to produce the products that the rest of us in the world enjoy.

Or how multi-million dollar fortunes have been generated from the sale of organs from living people in the most repugnant and appalling form of commerce ever witnessed in human history.

I discovered the true intention of the CCP in China's gloomy prisons and labor camps, which is none other than to destroy the values that represent the most benevolent and noble attributes of humankind.

Investigative reports from 2006 by Canadians David Kilgour and David Matas on organ harvesting of Falun Dafa practitioners in China revealed to me the gigantic scale of this genocide.

Their interviews with practitioners who had been arrested and imprisoned in labor camps confirmed that while imprisoned, they were subject to medical health checks and blood tests, with the only plausible goal to murder them for their organs (Falun Dafa practitioners are regularly tortured so such tests are clearly not used to improve their health).

In Europe, the resolution on organ harvesting in China adopted by the European Parliament on December 12th, 2013, underlines the international community's concerns regarding these atrocities. The resolution asks that European countries pay attention to and condemn the abuses of forced organ harvesting in China. It also urges the European Union to conduct a full investigation to stop these crimes against humanity, and requests the release of all prisoners of conscience in China, including Falun Gong practitioners.

We must dismiss from our minds any barrier that limits us to consider these crimes as matters of state, or as political or internal affairs of another country. This is precisely the game that those who are guilty of genocide want us to play. They want the world to believe that state sovereignty trumps human dignity and life, universal freedoms and international laws.

Sixty-six years after its inception, we remember the Preamble to the Universal Declaration of Human Rights, adopted by the General Assembly of the United Nations on December 10th, 1948, after the end of the Second World War:

> *"Whereas disregard and contempt for human rights have resulted in barbarous acts which have outraged the conscience of mankind, and the advent of a world in which human beings shall enjoy freedom of speech and belief."*

Reading this preamble breaks my heart, knowing that one of the countries that signed it—as well as being a member of the United Nations and holding the privilege of veto in the UN Security Council—is, under the leadership of the CCP, responsible for the murder of more than 80 million people.

Reading this preamble I cannot help but to remember with deep emotion all the victims of the brutality of the CCP dictatorship; the innocent children, the elderly and all the men and women who, since the Party first came to power in 1949, have been tortured and killed for their beliefs. I am devastated by all the millions of Falun Gong practitioners in China whose happy and peaceful lives have been destroyed by this evil cult whose purpose is to destroy truthfulness, compassion and tolerance, turning the earth into a living hell.

I believe that not one of the articles declared in the Universal Declaration of Human Rights have been fulfilled nor found protection or coverage in China under CCP rule. I clearly affirm this statement with the evidence of those that have tried to bring to justice the notorious leaders of the CCP for their crimes of genocide and torture. I affirm this with the conviction that the

Chinese people are suffering from the greatest and most terrible dictatorship in the history of mankind.

All the platitudes, propaganda, lies and deceit that the CCP uses in its international relations have a common denominator when it comes to the issue of human rights: The manner in which the Chinese government treats its own people, Chinese officials insist, is an internal affair, not a political matter subject to analysis by or discussion with sovereign states.

These are the excuses made by the perpetrators of genocide in their engagement with Western leaders, who fear losing business arrangements, trade agreements and any economic advantages that come with a stable international relationship.

In light of such pressures that democratic leaders face, only moral values, ethics and the human spirit can prevail and reveal the truth. The questions are clear:

Do we silently accept and become accomplices of those accused of genocide in exchange for economic agreements? Does that not make us co-responsible for the genocide, torture and the crime of large-scale organ harvesting?

Should we accept that this genocide is a matter of sovereignty for the CCP, which has the authority over the Chinese people to direct the affairs of state in a sovereign manner?

Have we perhaps forgotten our commitments made in the Universal Declaration of Human Rights? Have human beings become objects subject to the arbitrary decision of their leaders?

"Torture is not considered by international law as a function of a head of state," affirmed Lord Nicholls on November 25, 1998 in the House of Lords during the process of Pinochet's extradition from Spain to England. We must not forget the evil game of the CCP, which manipulates the truth and aims to prevent all of us from discovering the reality of today's most egregious humanitarian crimes.

It is evident that this genocide of mass torture and murder committed since 1999 cannot, under any circumstance, be regarded as merely a political affair, a matter of state sovereignty, and certainly not, as the CCP would have us believe, an internal affair. We are talking about the most heinous crimes against humanity, a persecution of 100 million people, and in face of these crimes we cannot permit ourselves to negotiate. We can only have the courage and dignity to tell the Chinese Communist dictatorship that human beings are not a commodity, that they are not simply piece of meat that can be cut up and sold to the highest bidder.

International institutions and organizations, democratic governments and parliaments, are simply groups of people who make decisions; they have feelings, opinions and values, and they are the ones whose hearts can change the reality of our world. It is as simple as this: Breaking the silence on genocide saves human lives.

From these pages I am appealing to individuals, not institutions, not to position or rank, not to organizations, but to the heart of each person who has a responsibility to both the national and international public. You are the ones who can stop this terrible atrocity and who can use your conscience to convey the reality of what is happening in China under the dictatorship of the CCP. The great suffering of these victims does not only stem from physical or mental torture, but from the impotence of ignorance. It is therefore essential to convey the truth to people around the globe, to share our knowledge and to ensure that all people are aware of these terrible acts against humanity.

These are the most serious crimes against humanity. Our silence and indifference to these crimes allows the perpetrators to continue without reservation. Are we not giving permission to these crimes? Are we not transmitting a message that these heinous crimes have no consequence? Are we not promoting new perpetrators of genocide and torture to emerge as these crimes go unpunished?

All of us, especially those with public responsibilities, should recognize our own limitations on this earth—our time and opportunities for action are limited. We must take this moment to consider our choices and what we have or have not done to ensure a better world for all people. History will judge how we responded, or did not respond, to present circumstances.

Conclusion

The day will come when the noble Chinese people, originating from the most glorious civilization and culture of mankind, will blossom again, and leave behind the terror of brutality and cowardice of the Chinese Communist Party. The day will come when justice will be brought to Falun Dafa and its unwavering principles that could not be destroyed by the wickedness of the Party. And the day will come when harmony will return for all Chinese people, and they will regain their culture of 5,000 years, and justice and truth will return to the hearts of these good people. We just need to make sure that we are part of these important events and that we stand on the right side of history.

Section V

CULTURAL

A Look at the Different Journeys of a Divine Culture in China and Abroad through Chinese Classical Dance

By Vina Lee

I was born in mainland China in the early 1960s. My earliest memory coincided with the Cultural Revolution. I would occasionally overhear adults talking about someone who hanged themselves, someone was beaten up or some other incidents. At such a tender age, I could not make any sense of what the adults were talking about. All I understood was to be very careful when I went outside.

During those days, the only cultural entertainment programs in all of China were just eight Peking opera and Chinese ballet shows that praised the 'glory and achievements' of Mao Zedong and the Communist Party. They were the so-called "Eight Revolutionary Model Shows". Among them was a Chinese ballet titled *The White-Haired Girl*, with a dance segment called "The North Wind Blows". This was my introduction to dance. I taught myself too, since I had watched *The White-Haired Girl*, both the film and the live performances, countless times.

At that time throughout the country, regardless of whether it was by a professional art troupe (now called "song and dance ensemble") or an amateur propaganda team, no matter one's age and gender, the eight model shows were performed everywhere.

Life was completely inundated with the sights and sounds of the eight model shows. The Chinese phrase "every home and household knows it" is literally the case here. Everyone knew those shows. Furthermore, everyone could perform them. It was not voluntary though; it was mandatory.

Before the end of the Cultural Revolution, I gained admission to a song and dance ensemble and began studying dance full-time. Back then my father, who had worked in the arts but was forced by circumstances to change his career, was very unwilling to see his daughter becoming a professional dancer. He knew that art should be a true reflection and elevation of the heart. Without an honest inner world, real art would be absent. But during that time, no artist could engage in authentic artistic work. If you were to express true feelings of human nature from your heart, you would either be "beaten down" or locked up in prison. However, if you buried your conscience and "sang the praises for the Party", you would not deserve to be called an artist.

I grew up under the Communist Party's brainwashing propaganda, such as "people all over the world are living in hell-like misery; we Chinese are the happiest people in the world" or "the American imperialism is our enemy". We were taught to believe that without the Communist Party, it would be the end of us too. I once asked my mother, "Why are others' mothers Party members and you are not?" Mother said to me: "A person, who is not a Party member, is not necessarily a bad person." However, because of this one question from me, mother applied to join the Party against her will, just so I could hold my head up high. Years later, whenever she mentioned this matter, she would say: "If you hadn't asked me that question, I would not have joined the Party." In this world, only the love for her children can make a mother sacrifice and short change herself. Fortunately, soon after The Epoch Times published the editorial series *Nine Commentaries on the Communist Party*, mother promptly made a declaration to quit her Communist Party membership.

During the 1970s, Chinese dance training was based on a combination of Chinese classical dance and Cuban style ballet, which
was practically the only way dancers were taught throughout the
country. In China, all things existed to serve the Party; the will of
the Party overruled human nature. Instead of being a vessel for
the elevation of human conscience, art was the Party's window
dressing. Likewise, sports weren't for people's fitness and enjoy-
ment, but to save face for the Communist Party on the international stage. Following the eviction of the former Soviet Union
ballet specialists and the political campaigns of the "Great Cultural Revolution", by the early and mid 1970s the efforts of previous generations of Chinese dancers were laid to waste. Some
were persecuted ("if the Party wanted you dead, you wouldn't
survive"), some were exiled (sent away to rural labor camps), and
some had to change their vocation. A minority of them ignorant-
ly became the Party's propaganda tool and was involved in the
aforementioned "eight model shows".

The Cuban-style of ballet teaching was propagated under the
Communist dogma of "using the foreign to serve the domestic;
using the classic to serve the contemporary". The Chinese dance
form, including its original rich expressiveness and the difficult
techniques, were not reflected in the teaching and creation of
dance. They also failed to showcase the linear beauty and heavenly grace of ballet. The dance training and choreography were
full of affected praises for the Communist Party. The performers
felt that the shows were a charade and they themselves were a
sham. However, when immersed in such an environment they
were blinded and had no alternatives.

In fact, the essence of China's 5,000 years of divine culture is reflected in many ways. Chinese classical dance also has a history
of thousands of years. The Chinese characters for "dance" and

"martial arts" share the same pronunciation (*"wu"*), which in it-self is a manifestation of China's divine culture. Martial arts are for self-defense and combat. Their established movements cannot be altered or they will lose their practical effect; that is why af-ter being handed down for thousands of years, their movements have remained basically unchanged. When the ancient warriors performed in the imperial courts, they adapted the martial arts movements into dance. In addition, Chinese people's movements and gestures carry their unique character and bearing, which is imbued in and expressed through Chinese classical dance. By this ingenious way, the Chinese classical dance was preserved through the divine culture.

Many difficult movements in modern day gymnastics and ac-robatics were all derived from Chinese classical dance. Chinese dance is immensely expressive. There are no mechanical formu-lations. The dance can be used at will to tell a story and portray a character. Whether the movements are masculine, feminine, flu-id, structured, with amplitude or linear flow, they all are inclusive in the Chinese dance vocabulary.

When the Cultural Revolution ended in 1976, China entered the so-called "reform and open up" period. Some classical dance teachers returned to teaching and tried to recapture the unique characteristics of Chinese dance. Although they couldn't com-pletely walk away from the Cuban influence in the basic tech-niques training, they were able to adapt a relatively comprehen-sive set of teaching methods for the inner bearing. Whereas they thought the dance movements were "consolidated, developed, and evolved" from martial arts, traditional Chinese operas and theatre plays, it was in fact originated from the genius of the di-vine culture.

During those years, Beijing Dance Academy had its first college graduates of Chinese dance, ballet, and choreography. I was one of them.

With the nation's gate opened, the exchange between the dance community in China and abroad became increasingly frequent, yet most communications were focused on ballet and modern dance. A small number of Chinese dance teachers visited overseas, but they returned mostly with admiration of the modern elements. The entire dance community was enamored with the new and the foreign, and paid little attention to Chinese dance. Many turned to contemporary dance. Chinese ballet dancers frequently won awards in international ballet competitions. Many talents left China. Due to the lack of interest in Chinese classical dance, a large number of excellent Chinese classical dancers had to switch their dance style or retired prematurely.

During the "reform and open up" period, the Communist Party was also very worried about the introduction of Western values, which are contrary to the Communist ideology. Thus, they deliberately "opened up" in formality but not in substance, allowing people to pursue and indulge on all material things, but closed off anything spiritual.

In learning from the West, the Chinese dance community quickly mastered the techniques, but they were unable to convey the artistic essence and the authenticity of human nature in their works. This twisted combination of openness only in formality and lockdown in ideology resulted in the intentional and unintentional self-indulgence by the choreographers to escape reality, eventually mixing a variety of different dance vocabulary. They transformed Chinese dance into a chaotic fusion of all sorts of styles. Apart from the dance pieces that continued to grovel to the Party, the rest were almost all works of surrealism and ultra-modernism. Works were considered superior if the audiences did not comprehend them, and were deemed remarkable if the performers did not even understand the dance themselves. I once discussed post-1990s Chinese dance with a renowned Chinese dance director. He said: "Nowadays, even I, a dance professional, could not understand some of the dance in China. Let alone others. I've no idea what they are trying to do." Even when telling Chinese stories, dressed in traditional Chinese costumes, the dances display a distorted "Chinese style" produced by the deviated modern ideology.

Is it true that that no one appreciates the Chinese content? Or, is it that the Communist Party has been deliberately mutilating the divine culture?

Through its totalitarian rule, the Communist Party has forced atheism as a belief upon Chinese people. They abandoned the notion of "the good will be rewarded, and the wicked will be punished", and replaced it with "do whatever the Party tells you to do". The Party has the ultimate control. Growing up in this state of close-mindedness and under the Party's evil ideology, Chinese people unknowingly become dishonest, selfish and greedy. The trust between one and another is lost. Living in a heightened state of alertness and fear, they do not even know that this is not a natural way of life. After 5,000 years of civilization, what has been destroyed were not only the physical treasures and artifacts, but also the most fundamental—moral beliefs.

After I migrated to Australia in 1998, I was very fortunate to come across *Falun Dafa*, a cultivation practice guided by the Chinese Buddha school tenets of "truthfulness, compassion and forbearance". Its traditional spiritual teachings promptly led me to look at myself and things around me with a fresh perspective. To my surprise, those Chinese things I did not appreciate before, such as traditional Chinese landscape paintings, appeared in a new light in front of my eyes. An apparently simple painting depicting the tranquil lifestyle of the ancient people vividly illustrated the philosophy of "harmony between heaven and man". I lamented how much I had lost in the past!

In 2003 I accepted an invitation from the New York-based New Tang Dynasty Television to work on its *2004 New Year Gala* show. I encountered a number of overseas Chinese artists in the United States and discovered that we shared very similar experiences: we grew up in China, acquired professional skills under the Communist Party culture, realized our distorted ways after living abroad for a number of years, and came to cherish our ancestral culture and heritage. We have a common goal: to showcase the authentic, profound Chinese traditional culture on stage through performing arts.

Later, I was privileged to join Shen Yun Performing Arts Company (*"shen yun"* can be translated as divine beings dancing), whose mission is to revive the 5,000 years of China's divine culture mainly through high quality professional Chinese dance performances.

Since its establishment in 2006, Shen Yun Performing Arts has presented brand new performances every year and toured to hundreds of cities around the world. Shen Yun shows, consist primarily of pure Chinese classical song and dance in captivating short pieces, feature stories of historical Chinese figures, myths and legends. The graceful female dances are as beautiful as heavenly maidens; the masculine male dances use masterful techniques to showcase the spirit of Chinese dance to the audience. Shen Yun music is performed with unique Chinese instruments integrated with the Western orchestra. The East and the West is perfectly harmonized and the music is in impeccable unison with the dancers on stage, highlighting the integral bond between dance and music. The Shen Yun costumes, their colors, styles, and fabrics are astounding. The animated digital 3D backdrop uses modern technology to enhance a traditional stage.

With several hundred performances each year, Shen Yun has

brought to the audience a feast for the eyes and also an uplifting spirit. The audiences, in return, respond with applause and tears to show their appreciation of Shen Yun artists and their tremendous dedication.

Shen Yun artists not only need to have high level techniques, but are also expected to abide by the divine principles of "truthfulness, compassion, forbearance" in morals and conduct. Thus, a performer's movements and music are naturally rooted with innate goodness and purity. In the same token, they embody the concepts of a divine culture, such as "heaven and man in unity", "strength and softness in balance", and "internal and external in harmony". One cannot fake true beauty, and virtue does not rest on the surface. A person who is beautiful from within to the outside, is intriguing to watch and admire.

As a result of my involvement in Shen Yun performances, my understanding of China's divine culture deepened and I had an opportunity to rediscover and re-learn pure Chinese classical dance. China's 5,000 years of civilization is so immensely rich, it provides an inexhaustible source of materials and inspiration. It encompasses a multitude of human principles and universal values. Thus, China's divine culture does not only belong to China's wealth, but is also a treasure of the world.

The deviated will not defeat the righteous. Good will eventually overcome evil. This is a God given faith. Chinese classical dance is not just an art form. Its inner spirit reflects the values of a divine culture. A truly accomplished Chinese classical dancer must have this quality and bearing.

I feel an overwhelming sense of fulfillment that *Shen Yun Performing Arts* is based in the United States and presents genuine Chinese dance to the world. I also believe that in experiencing the spectacular Shen Yun shows, the world's audiences will benefit from its uplifting and transcending spirit.

Under Shen Yun's Glaring Brilliance the Chinese Communist Party is in an Awkward Position

By Yang Senhong

A lost civilization is revived! This was the thought that flashed across my mind the first time I saw the Shen Yun performance. Afterwards I read on Shen Yun's website the exact same statement, I realized that there are still people making valiant efforts to prove that the ancient empire (but now morally depraved) had once been grand and virtuous. The name "Shen Yun" clearly conveys a natural instinct of valuing heaven and earth in awe and reverence. The belief that Gods exist communicates a kind of gratitude with a spiritual mindset. The dedication of spreading such virtues and of giving people a sense of warmth that is untarnished, precious and tranquil. All these are nonexistent in the Chinese Communist Party, (CCP or the Party) its leaders are declared atheists who have already turned the Party into a living hell of evil spirits with a despicable personality that is insincere, devoid of goodness and without mercy. Several thousand years of Chinese civilization with its simple but refined cultural heritage, in the course of less than a half-century, under the Party's revolution—have all been reduced to a lifeless trunk and a pile of ashes. Today, the real "Cultural China" is what Du Fu describes in his poem: "the country lies in ruins although the mountains and rivers remain. When spring comes, vegetation still grows." The vast land of China is already not the same old "Cultural China". If Shen Yun did not exist and did not tour the world for several years, the global memory of the 21st century would not have any impression of a "Cultural China." Since 1949, "Communist China" has brought nothing to the world—but disasters, gloom, threats, war and barbarism.

Some say, to date, that Taiwan has preserved the "Chinese culture." This saying is not completely accurate. What is accurate is that Taiwan has preserved many precious cultural heritages in the Taipei National Palace Museum. Because fortunately back then, some people with foresight took the trouble to relocate them to Taiwan, thus saving them from catastrophe. Furthermore, it's accurate to say that the basic belief in the Chinese culture, has become part of people's lives in Taiwan. More accurate information is that Taiwan, in the second half of the 19th century, had already experienced direct exposure to the world history. For more than a century, the influence from the South Island Aboriginal culture, along with the influx of cultures from the Netherlands, Spain, and Japan, the culture of the Taiwanese people formed a melting pot that is clearly distinct from that of the original "Chinese culture." Viewed from the perspective of cultural anthropology, strictly speaking, Taiwan is not part of China, but China is indeed a very important part for Taiwan. However, in this instance the "China" that we are referring to is the "China," which the Communist Party has never interposed or participated in. Taiwan's fate and the spread of Shen Yun have a very similar pattern of development and karmic relationship. In the process of continuous oppression by the Communist regime, Taiwan has never surrendered its basic elements of "Chinese culture." For example, regarding the written Chinese characters, the Taiwanese have preserved what is often called the "traditional" style of written Chinese characters. These scripts were handed down since ancient times and have not succumbed to the Communist regime's simplified Chinese version, which has in many respects become alienated from ancient Chinese culture. However, Taiwan is constantly in the process of innovating and internationalizing its freedom to continue its coexistence alongside world civilization with a Taiwanese-style civilization and culture. Many Chinese who visit Taiwan are fond of the place. They all think they are finally face to face with what the rumors say is the "ancient civilization" of "cultural China." This is a severe misunderstanding. In fact, what they are exposed to is "Taiwan's innovative civilization," that contains "Chinese culture".

Shen Yun's development is similarly walking the path of "Taiwan's innovative culture." It can be said to be a "free China innovative culture." Regardless of what kind of "culture" Shen Yun follows, as long as it remains outside of the borders of "Communist China," it is possible to plant its root and grow. Shen Yun has been developed in the United States, with many performers who are American-born Chinese, with no option to return to China or even tour China for the time being. Moreover, Shen Yun is a kind of "Chinese culture" that soars by riding on the wings of Western aesthetics. Therefore, the art is perceived to be originally from creation, illustrating how people admire and revere God. Depiction of the bright side of humanity was added after the Renaissance. Such a development is also something that "Communist China" cannot imitate, no matter how hard it tries. The reason is that when there is no faith, there cannot be accomplishments in the arts.

There is a passage in Shen Yun's website that is capable of conveying succinctly this wonderful combination of Eastern and Western civilizations: "From the goddesses in the Dunhuang Grottoes to the paintings in the ceiling of the Sistine Chapel, these immortal works not only display superb skills, but also arouse respect and reverence, because they demonstrate praises toward God. Today, Shen Yun's artists, through practicing Falun Gong, are infusing and reflecting God's divine essence in the works they produce."

This should be the treasure trove of secrets of Shen Yun's success. These secrets are impossible to be counterfeited by the CCP's so called "arts groups," with their gaudy-style performances. Thus, this contemporary "Chinese Renaissance" is clearly distinct from the CCP. However, Shen Yun embraces and maintains the essence of its heritage. In recent years, the CCP has invested a vast budget establishing "Confucius Institutes" in foreign universities in an attempt to compete for cultural interpretation, but these "institutes" are eventually closed down when it comes to light, that the CCP is merely using cultural exchange in name. These so called "classes" are engaging party agents for spying and infiltration activities in Western education. Even the name *Confucius*, our national icon, the most revered "wise teacher," is being exploited as a special agent by the CCP. For a regime that represents the destruction of civilization and culture, it is of course impossible to gain the world's respect.

Shen Yun Performing Arts Orchestra directs Western orchestral instruments, this part of the ensemble are the foundation, while the melodic components are formed by the erhu, pipa, flute and other traditional Chinese instruments. The musical outcome produced is both harmonious and moving. Not only are the Western symphony's broad and brilliant momentum highlighted, but ethnic heritage and unique style of performing arts in Chinese civilization is resonated. Chinese dance includes classical as well as ethnic and folk dances. The dance style of *Shen Yun Performing Arts* is mainly rooted in the basic skills training of Chinese classical dance. It also performs a certain number of ethnic and folk dances, each of which embodies the different mindset and aesthetic characteristics of vast ethnic groups in China. Chinese classical dance has a history of thousands of years. It encompasses the wisdom of every dynasty, forming the aesthetic consciousness passed down from generation to generation. Early Chinese classical dance was mainly performed in the Emperor's palace, but it was also preserved and spread in ancient opera theaters. It consisted of very difficult movements, abundant skills and a myriad of expressions. Chinese ethnic and folk dances, handed down in many regions from over 50 minority groups, are a rich conglomeration of traditions with very distinct characteristic and style. Shen Yun performances display superb dancing skills, a unique mix of Chinese and Western composition, stunning costumes, and dynamic animated backdrop designs. They also underscore the traditional concept that includes the bond between the divine and humanity—honor of the divine, acceptance of one's own destiny, the retribution of good and evil, the practice of the five virtues, "benevolence, righteousness, propriety, wisdom, faithfulness," and others. The virtues at the core of this blended innate concept is not only incompatible with the philosophy of the CCP, but also something the CCP wanted to get rid of for years, right from the start.

Over the years, the CCP considered Shen Yun an intense enemy. The first year, when Shen Yun had only one company, the CCP dispatched around 60 troupes to perform for overseas audiences, in order to compete with Shen Yun. This CCP tactic was also an attempt to ensure Shen Yun would not survive financially under the onslaught. What actually happened was, the CCP not only exhausted a lot of manpower and squandered a lot of resources, but its own troupes also suffered devastating defeat and returned home in disgrace. "The First Emperor" the opera, directed by famed director Zhang Yimou, was denounced by American critics. For the ensuing years, the CCP engaged all of its domestic troupes to be involved in bringing about Shen Yun's demise. The CCP's scheme was to urge all performing groups to go abroad to set up shows in close proximity, with the principal intent to use underhanded tactics to compete for the market, and create disturbances. At the same time, the CCP consulates were all directed to contact the theaters where Shen Yun was contracted to perform, slandering and vilifying the performing arts company. There were ludicrous demands made to theater managers to cancel their legal agreements with Shen Yun, and threats made about political and economic relationships between the two countries as a form of blackmail and intimidation. The CCP failed to recognize that its approach is in sharp contrast to those of Western democracies. The CCP habitually uses the methodology employed by gangsters and mafia to force theaters in Western societies to comply. Ironically this results in more rejection and CCP representatives being the laughing stock of the West. After years of cooperation with Shen Yun, theater managers all around the world have come to respect and understand Shen Yun and Falun Gong, and they are quite repulsed by the CCP's intrusive interference. The CCP, at the end of its wits, like a donkey having exhausted its tricks, actually stooped so low as to resort to sabotaging Shen Yun's buses. There was an instance where the Shen Yun tour bus had its tires slashed and an unknown fluid was injected into the gas tank to cause damage. Such acts were an example of methods used to disrupt Shen Yun tours.

The CCP's evil actions have only validated the inevitability of Shen Yun's historical role. The CCP is struggling to survive and is blanketed by Shen Yun's undisputed success. Not only is the regime's legitimacy of ruling China questionable, its core existence is also in distress. The world's people will come to realize that "Communist China" is not the center, the heart of "Cultural China," but the "Lost Paradise," a wasteland on the brink of destruction and ruins. Shen Yun resembles the sun at high noon. Under Shen Yun's brand, "Communist China" has no escape, and it will be reduced to being "culturally illiterate." The lies, at the dead end of its resources, and reduced to picking up ruins, will be the fate of Communist China.

About the Authors

Michel Wu, was a reporter for China's state-run Xinhua International News Department and is the former director of the Radio France Internationale's (RFI) Mandarin language service.

Clive Ansley, BA, MA, LL.B, and LL.M, graduated from the University of British Columbia, University of Windsor and the University of London and is a Canadian human rights lawyer who practiced law in Mainland China for 14 years. He speaks and reads in Chinese and has managed over 300 litigation cases in Chinese courts. As a former professor of Chinese History, Civilization, and Law he provides international expert analysis on China's law. Mr. Ansley taught at the University of Windsor, the University of British Columbia, the Law Faculty of Shanghai's Fudan University, and the Law Faculty of Shanghai's Jiaotong University

Chang Chin-Hwa, Ph.D., graduated from the University of Iowa, currently Senior Professor of Graduate Institute of Journalism, National Taiwan University. She is an award winning teacher and a current board member of the Chinese Communication Society (CCS).

David Kilgour, J.D., former Canadian Secretary of State for Asia-Pacific, senior member of the Canadian parliament and nominee for the Nobel Peace Prize for his work related to the investigation of forced organ harvesting crimes against Falun Gong practitioners in China. He was a Crowne Prosecutor and longtime expert commentator of the CCP's persecution of Falun Gong and human rights issues in Africa. He co-authored Bloody Harvest: Killed For Their Organs and La Mission au Rwanda.

Yuan Hongbing, one of the most internationally renowned Chinese dissidents, is a novelist and philosopher in exile, famous for his poetry and political activism. He is a law graduate of Beijing University and became the head of the School of Criminal Procedural law at Beijing University. Yuan served as China interim government congressman and is the founder and first committee member of The Chinese Cultural Freedom Movement and first chair of China Federal Revolution Party. He is editor-in-chief of fireofliberty.org and is based in Australia.

Zhang Tianliang (Shujia Gong), Ph.D., former adjunct professor of George Mason University, is Dean of the Department of Liberal Arts and Sciences at the New York based Feitian Academy of the Arts. He is a popular columnist at the Epoch Times and senior commentator at New Tang Dynasty Television and guest commentator at Voice of America. He is the author of China's Path to Peaceful Transition.

Edward McMillan-Scott, former vice president and senior member of the European Parliament, is the founder of the European Instrument for Democracy and Human Rights (EIDHR), and received the Medal of Honour by the European Inter-University Centre (EIUC) for Human Rights and Democratization. He is a long-time observer of China's human rights situation with a particular interest on Falun Gong and Chinese human rights attorney Gao Zhisheng.

Xia Yiyang (Heng He), is an expert on Chinese politics, economy, sociology, and history and has extensive research publications on these topics. He also specializes in pathophysiology and immunology in China and the United States, and is a high profile presenter at international conferences.

Katrina Lantos Swett, J.D., Ph.D., is the former Chair and now committee member of the United States Commission on International Religious Freedom (USCIRF). In 2008, she established the Lantos Foundation for Human Rights and Justice and serves as its President and CEO. She teaches human rights and American foreign policy at Tufts University.

Teng Biao, human rights lawyer and former professor at China University of Political Science and Law, is currently a visiting scholar at Harvard Law School. He is the founder of the New Citizens Movement and Director of China Against Death Penalty in Beijing. A long time China rights activist Teng participated in the cases of Sun Zhigang, Hu Jia, Chen Guangcheng, Gao Zhisheng, Cao Shunli, and Falun Gong cases.

Wu Huilin, Ph.D., a former National Taiwan University Economics professor, is a visiting scholar at Chicago University Economics Department, researcher at Chung-Hua Institution for Economic Research, professor at Shih Hsin University and professor at the Graduate Institute of Technological & Vocational Education at National Taipei University of Technology. He authored "The Surface and Truth of China's Economic Reform," and published over 100 scholarly articles and current affairs commentaries.

Torsten Trey, M.D., Ph.D., is the founder, Executive Director of Doctors Against Forced Organ Harvesting, a Nobel Peace Prize nominated NGO based in the United States. Dr. Trey and David Matas jointly edited "State Organs—Transplant Abuse in China." He is a notable researcher, an international expert with extensive publications on unethical organ procurement and transplant abuse in China.

Kirk C. Allison, Ph.D., director of the Program in Human Rights and Health of the Center of Holocaust and Genocide Studies at the University of Minnesota School of Public Health. Dr. Allison has provided testimony to the Congressional House Committee on Foreign Relations concerning organ harvesting in China.

Huang Shiwei, M.D., attending physician at National Taiwan University Hospital, Vice Chairman and Spokesperson of Taiwan International Care Association for Organ Transplants, has interviewed many patients, middlemen, and transplant surgeons in Taiwan. A longtime observer of China's source of transplant organs, Dr. Huang is dedicated to ending illegal organ procurement practices in China.

David Matas, awarded Canadian human rights lawyer and appointed member of the Order of Canada, serves on the board of directors of The International Centre for Human Rights and Democratic Development of Canada. In 2010 he was nominated for the Nobel Peace Prize for his work related to the investigation of forced organ harvesting crimes against Falun Gong practitioners in China. Matas co-authored with David Kilgour Bloody Harvest: The Killing of Falun Gong for their Organs and co-edited State Organs—Transplant Abuse in China with Dr. Torsten Trey.

Theresa Chu (Wanqi Chu), lawyer and Taiwan Falun Gong Human Rights Lawyer Group spokesperson, is a legal consultant for DAFOH in Asia. Ms. Chu has assisted Falun Gong practitioners in the lawsuits against Jiang Zemin, Luo Gan, and other high-ranking CCP officials. She also has represented Falun Gong in the lawsuits of ten CCP officials for the crime of genocide and is the co-author of The Chinese Book of Living and Dying.

Carlos Iglesias Jimenez, Spanish human rights lawyer representing Falun Gong practitioners in lawsuits, successfully prosecuted Jiang Zemin and four other high-ranking CCP officials with crimes of genocide and torture. He is the Europe Director of the Human Rights Law Foundation. He spoke at the UN Human Rights Council in Geneva informing its members about the persecution of Falun Gong.

Vina Lee, is based in New York and Company Director of Shen Yun Performing Arts and President of the Feitian Academy of the

Arts, Born in China before the Cultural Revolution, she studied dance and was the first generation graduate from Beijing Dance Academy. She was a principal artist with Guangdong Dance Theatre and relocated to Australia.

Yang Senhong, senior Taiwanese journalist, human rights activist and program host at Radio Taiwan International, founded and operated by the Taiwanese government, is founder of the NGO Taiwan Association for Human Rights (TAHR). He was editor-in-chief at Taiwan News and director of Taiwan News Financial Weekly.

Torsten Trey, MD, PhD, founder and executive director of the medical ethics advocacy group, Doctors Against Forced Organ Harvesting, (DAFOH) which has been nominated for Nobel Peace Prize, is among those who lead the global movement against forced organ harvesting in China. Considered a leading expert in the field, Dr. Trey has co-authored books and published widely in medical journals on this topic. An international speaker, Dr. Trey was recently featured in the award-winning documentary, *Human Harvest*. He is co-editor of the book, *State Organs: Transplant Abuse in China*.

Theresa Chu is an international human rights lawyer. Since the onset of the persecution against Falun Gong in 1999, she has defended victims on a pro bono basis, and is actively involved in litigation to bring suit against former Chinese Party, Chief Jiang Zemin, and other CCP officials involved in organ harvesting crimes. An influential leader, Attorney Chu supported changes to human rights laws in Taiwan as adviser to the Taiwanese government. She is an expert lecturer, speaking before international government officials, human rights organizations and members of parliament about human rights concerns and the collective lawsuits from countries all over the world by Falun Gong victims.

Made in the USA
Middletown, DE
20 May 2017